Heartfelt

The Inspirational Story Of Medha Anup Jalota

Bharathi S Pradhan

OM
Om Books International

Published in 2013 by

Om Books International

Corporate & Editorial Office
A-12, Sector 64, Noida 201 301
Uttar Pradesh, India
Phone: +91 120 477 4100
Email: editorial@ombooks.com
Website: www.ombooksinternational.com

Sales Office
4379/4B, Prakash House, Ansari Road
Darya Ganj, New Delhi 110 002, India
Phone: +91 11 2326 3363, 2326 5303
Fax: +91 11 2327 8091
Email: sales@ombooks.com
Website: www.ombooks.com

ISBN: 978-93-80070-15-5

Printed at Thomson Press (I) Ltd.

10 9 8 7 6 5 4 3 2 1

Bharathi S Pradhan, currently the editor of *The Film Street Journal* and a Sunday columnist with *The Telegraph*, has edited *Star & Style*, *Lehren*, *Showtime*, *Savvy* (Consulting Editor) and *Movie,* besides writing for a wide variety of publications, including *Eve's Weekly*, *Femina*, *The Free Press Journal*, *Mid-day* and *Reader's Digest*. Bharathi was the first print-medium journalist to face the camera for *Lehren*, India's first video magazine.

Apart from journalism, she has scripted a documentary on *Mughal-e-Azam*, ideated a serial for Balaji Telefilms and written the screenplay for a feature film. She has also been assigned to write an exclusive coffee-table book on legendary filmmaker, BR Chopra.

Bharathi has been Chairperson of the National Awards and on the jury of the Indian Television Academy Awards, the DY Patil Achiever's Awards and GIFA in Dubai.

Valentine Lover, her first novel, was a best-seller. Her critically-acclaimed *Colas, Cars & Communal Harmony* documented the lives of celebrities who have had highly successful inter-faith marriages.

Married to a chartered accountant, Bharathi has a son and lives in Mumbai.

Attractive Medha Gujral and renowned filmmaker, Shekhar Kapur, ended their high-profile marriage in a Tis Hazari divorce court in New Delhi.

Bhajan Samrat Anup Jalota had two infamously unsuccessful marriages behind him.

When Medha and Anup met, a series of failed relationships and a passion for music was the only common ground between them. But as man and woman, they became inseparable. The arrival of precious baby Aryaman multiplied their happiness. However, this unbridled bliss was rudely truncated when Medha was diagnosed with a debilitating congenital heart disease in 2000.

Since then the Jalotas have seen it all – a chordae of her mitral valve cut by mistake in a US hospital, an emergency open-heart surgery, a life-saving heart transplant and a hospital check-in scheduled in New York on, believe it or not, 9/11 in 2001.

But, despite a decade and more of dwindling health, near-encounters with death, emotional oscillations and spiralling medical bills, Anup and Medha celebrate every moment of their life together.

Heartfelt: The Inspirational Story Of Medha Anup Jalota is a living statement of how the mind can battle, even heal the body, when medical science gives up on you.

Contents

1. The Mind Can Talk To The Body 1
2. If The Spirit Is Willing, The Flesh Responds 6
3. Anup's Chant: Happiness Is Therapeutic 12
4. Shekhar Kapur's Robust Bride, Medha 32
5. A Privileged Childhood 35
6. L'affaire Shekhar Kapur 66
7. Anup, The Anchor 76
8. The Heart Breaks Down 86
9. The Kidneys Fail 110
10. An Anxious Family Notes The Change 121
11. The Magic Returns 139
12. Kidney Watch 147
13. The Support System 149
14. Hope 2012 197

1

The Mind Can Talk To The Body

When his celebrity-patient was first wheeled into Hinduja Hospital, Mumbai, the much-respected nephrologist was not pleased. Dr Jatin P Kothari at Mumbai's prestigious PD Hinduja National Hospital & Medical Centre, had neither the time nor the temperament to tolerate the tantrums of the rich and the famous.

Besides, this was a case wrought with complications. Medha Jalota, the attractive third wife of celebrated singer Anup Jalota, was a rare patient, right from the start. In India, Dr Kothari had not dealt, so far, with a heart-transplant survivor whose kidneys were rapidly failing, forcing her to face two stark options: to teeter between two worlds as a unique multi-organ transplant patient or to give up and accept the inevitable. There was very little hope the experienced surgeon could hold out to her.

When Medha struck back at doomsday prescriptions with a magical recovery, Dr Kothari had to rethink many of his beliefs. This was neither a demanding celebrity nor a vacuous wilting willow. In fact, Medha altered the portrait of an ideal patient many times over with a sensible head for maintaining her medical files, which she updated with precision, and she coped with her precarious ailments with a spunk and spirit that had no known references to anything in the medical tomes.

Miracles in Medha's life were also witnessed, recorded and explained professionally by Dr Alok Chopra, MD of Aashlok, a small boutique hospital in New Delhi. Dr Chopra who had watched Medha since her robust days in Delhi, analysed, "I think the primary reason she has carried on is her basic intrinsic nature which is extremely positive and her intense desire to live life to the fullest. I think that has been her main driving force at all times, a strong addiction to life."

He explained with the wisdom of experience, "We often see patients going into mental depression and letting go. When we say letting go, it means many physical, chemical things happen in the body.

"Today we have a new, or a relatively new science called Psychoneuroimmunology. It means that a thought that enters the mind is like a chemical time bomb which gets transmitted to the rest of the body through a system of neuro-transmitters or neuro-peptides or neuro-chemicals. Each of these neuro-chemicals or neuro-peptides has a particular effect on the functioning of the body. This has been identified but is difficult to explain in scientific detail. Suffice it to say, the fact that the body and mind can talk to each other is no longer a myth or a hocus-pocus phenomenon. It has been proven that through the system of neuro-transmitters, our minds and our thoughts are actually translated into our physiology.

"We can now correlate people's positivity to their recovery and how much their positive attitude impacts the ultimate outcome of an illness. It is absolutely fantastic that people with positive frames of mind, people who have great attitudes, great relationships, something meaningful to do in life, can ride through an illness with a lot more grace than those who have a negative attitude. Even with minor illnesses, those who are negative in their approach attract misfortune from all corners, on the relationship, social and environmental fronts."

The doctor succinctly summed this up with the refreshing disclosure, "No longer can we say that having a positive attitude is just a façade. It is truly a bio-chemical and biological phenomenon that recovery is directly proportionate to our attitude."

Medha's refusal to accept defeat or to go into depression, no matter how dire the prescriptions and predictions, gave new faith even to her doctors. Dr Chopra marvelled, "It is miraculous that each time she falls, Medha uses the same ground to get up again. I'm confident now that these miracles are possible. As doctors or medical care-givers, we are not creating the miracles, we are only watching them happen."

Intriguingly, much of Medha's miraculous recoveries were directly linked to the curative presence of Dr Alan Gass, former Medical Director of New York Mount Sinai's Heart Transplant Program, a god-send who gave her a new heart in 2001; a man who went beyond the precision of medical science to weave intangible visual imagery into the healing process. It was wonderful to watch Medha scale high and fast in recovery when Dr Gass was her patron-doctor. It was also a disturbing coincidence that in his absence, she would slump, her health would actually plummet as it did in 2008-2009. The huge extremes in her condition that swung from the miraculously positive to the despairingly negative, had to be traced to the unyielding hold her mind had over her body.

Dr Gass, now at Westchester Medical Center to treat patients with end-stage heart failure, was solemn as he observed, "The medical profession does not understand certain things. The medical profession is based on science which is something that you can see, you can add numbers to, take pictures of. Why medicine has never accepted the spiritual aspect of health is because it cannot be measured, you cannot take an X-ray of it, and I hate to say it but you cannot charge for it. You cannot charge to help or improve somebody's spirit."

According to Dr Gass, his fraternity in the US was largely opposed to spirituality. Doctors saw miracles happening in their patients but they chose to ignore them.

"I can tell you many, many stories of how my wife or I have worked with patients doing mental imagery," continued Dr Gass. "And we have seen some unbelievable results that had nothing to do with medicine. If you do 100 transplants, not everybody is going to recover the same way. They are all getting the same bright, shiny new hearts and the same treatment but the recovery has something to do with the patient's spirit.

"I have seen tumours go away, I have seen mental imagery work wonders in my own life. I had broken my hip and it healed in a month with mental imagery. There are books written on it. Gerald Epstein is a world expert whose book *Healing Into Immortality* explains how mental imagery can help people. So there are many aspects outside medicine that we don't understand."

Medha presented a unique case where a heart transplant survivor was on dialysis for over four years, mood-swinging between a heart-breaking wait for a kidney donor and not wanting to go in for another organ transplant.

Dr Kothari, who oversaw her dialysis and monitored her while she awaited a kidney donor, was the best person to answer one crucial, critical question – even if Medha were to get a donor and undergo a kidney transplant, what were her chances of survival?

"It's a difficult question," he replied. "If she goes through the kidney transplant and does well in the first six to eight weeks, then her chances will be good as long as the heart lasts. On an average a heart transplant patient survives between 10 and 15 years. That's just an average, some have survived beyond 15 and some have succumbed before 10. Going by the average, Medha hopefully has another five to six years of the heart to go on and I'm sure the kidney will continue to work during that period. Doing a second heart transplant is going to be an extremely difficult proposition. As of now, we have never discussed that openly with her. She knows the difficulty it will entail, that's probably why even she doesn't want to talk about it right now. We will take one step at a time, and with a kidney transplant, we can hope for at least an additional five to six years of good quality life. Maybe by that time we will have something better in science to help her."

Or maybe, Medha will help herself again and spring another pleasant surprise on her care-givers, as she did at the dawn of the new millennium in Mussoorie where it all began.

2

If The Spirit Is Willing, The Flesh Responds

It was a wonderful break for the city-bred group of Mumbaikars who woke up to the fragrance of a crisp Mussoorie air and the sound of soothing *bhajans* (devotional songs). When the idyllic holiday began, there was little to indicate how sombrely it would wind up.

Medha's cousin, Prem Kishen (head honcho, Cinevista, fondly called 'Junior') and wife Sunita Malhotra clearly remembered the vacation in the hill station of Mussoorie in north India where the first chapter of the saga was unwittingly written. Medha, Anup, Sunita, Junior and members of both their families had gathered in Mussoorie in May, 2000, for a leisurely holiday away from their regular city routine.

Sunita and Junior chimed almost in unison, "Yes, of course we remember that trip but at that time we didn't realise the enormity of Medha's condition. We couldn't have foretold just how complicated it was all going to be."

It hit them without any prior indication, although Prem Kishen and Sunita were aware that Medha had the medical history of a degenerative heart muscle condition.

Sunita acknowledged, "We knew that Medha may not be able to have a child and that she had a problem with her heart in her childhood but we never thought of it as a serious threat to her life because we had always seen her so healthy. In Mussoorie too, she would go for walks with all of us. But towards the end of the trip, we found her tiring easily. She couldn't walk much, she would want to rest."

It was there that Medha developed breathlessness and Junior had to find less strenuous paths for her daily treks.

Prem Kishen said, "We had no inkling that it had anything to do with the deterioration of her heart condition. We never dreamt it would be a problem of this magnitude."

Sunita re-lived the quick succession of events thereafter. "When we got back from Mussoorie, her condition worsened. Her stomach began to bloat and she would look like a six months pregnant woman. Soon her heart condition was detected and for months thereafter, she was in and out of hospital."

"But she is such a fighter," both agreed. "All through the last 11 years, we have never seen her cry or even grumble over what she was going through."

Sunita also reported, "After her heart transplant, we happened to be in New York and we stayed with her for a few days. Post-surgery, she was keen to live in a nice apartment with a beautiful view. Anup found her just the right place; it was so lovely, overlooking a river. He has always taken such good care of her."

Sunita paused to comment on the unbelievable equanimity of the couple who has never allowed adversity to weigh down its spirits. In the exhausting preamble before she could come home with a new heart, Medha had made two disheartening trips to the renowned Mayo Clinic in Rochester to get a correct diagnosis for her ailment.

Shivering at the coldness of it all, Sunita recollected, "They had a terrible setback at Mayo Clinic where they accidentally messed up her case. Anup and Medha chose to look forward instead of getting caught up in negativity. After that stint, Medha started losing weight and her condition really deteriorated. Before her heart transplant, all of us were extremely worried. But she fought back and came out of it, an admirable trait that she has demonstrated all through.

"Seven years after the heart transplant, when her kidneys failed in 2007, there were so many problems one after the other – breathlessness, water retention and the heart acting up – that we were worried again. More than 11 years later, to this day, it is only Medha's spirit that keeps getting her out of these dire complications."

Despite Medha's and Anup's round-the-clock buoyancy, those around the fast-sinking patient had their moments of doubt.

"That tension was always there," admitted Junior. "She was on the brink of slipping away many a time but always came around just when you were ready for the worst." He additionally observed, "Medha has always got fantastic support from Anup who gave her the strength to go on. They literally fought this out together. My admiration for the two of them is tremendous."

Where did this kind of fortitude and strength come from?

"Goodness counts," commented Sunita. "They are both very good human beings who have never harmed anybody. Medha figures in my daily prayers. We feel she has had more than her fair share of suffering. And she is still smiling and full of life."

That Medha put up a spirited fight each time adversity came visiting, was an observation made by friends, family and medical experts. Persistent positivity led to an incredibly tangible outcome, evinced both in Medha's own comeback each time, and in the manner their young son, Aryaman, grew up.

Junior voiced it when he pointed out, "Such critical situations could have taken a toll on their son. It is to their credit that they kept it all completely normal and Aryaman has grown into a lovely, secure child. You can tell from the way they have brought him up that Anup and Medha have done a fine job as parents, despite the life-threatening situations they have continuously battled."

The Jalota-Malhotra connection was almost karmic because it was also during Medha's prolonged and critical hospitalisation in the US that Anup hosted a programme for their company, Cinevista, every Sunday morning. "Yes, it was called *Dharam Aur Hum* for Star Plus," nodded Junior. "It was a beautiful show. He used to come from New York to Mumbai, tape a whole lot of episodes and create a bank for us before flying back to be with her. If you had met him then, you would have never guessed what he was going through. He kept himself calm and never showed any tension while hosting those programmes."

Sunita ruminated, "Even in the worst of times, Anup was always very confident that Medha would pull through and survive. We never saw him mope or indulge in any self-pity." Junior commented, "Even when talking about her illness, he would be absolutely calm."

"Medha was always practical and sensible," said Sunita "I have never seen her indulge in melodrama. For instance, she once had to wear a mask as a necessary precaution when she came over to our place. She did it in a matter-of-fact manner without making a spectacle of herself."

And there were crippling bills too. "She didn't have medical insurance, so all the years of intense treatment cost them more money than they could afford," Sunita shared. "All through, Anup has been constantly doing shows all over the world. It's an amazing story of how they have faced all this without ever complaining or cribbing.

"Medha would sometimes come over on a Sunday because mom (Prem Kishen's mother, late actress Bina Rai) used to spend the day with us. On the very last Sunday that mom spent with us, Medha was there too. We were leaving for Australia after that and Medha was going to the US. Mom passed away while we were in Australia. So Medha got to see her the Sunday before she died."

Junior looked at it from a man's perspective and observed appreciatively, "Anup has always taken great pains to ensure that Medha is comfortable. Because he would be flying up and down, post her heart transplant in New York, he got her the kind of apartment that would give her happiness. Every time he was away, which was rather often, he would make sure that Medha was not alone. He would arrange for a family member or a friend to be around her."

He added wistfully, "On that holiday in Mussoorie, all of us used to sing bhajans every morning."

Sunita perked up as she recalled, "What better way to wake up every day? Anup and Medha would do their *riyaaz* (practice) and sing in the mornings, and they would be joined by Junior. Then all of us would sing along and start the day. It was beautiful."

Junior remembered poignantly, "We had such a good time that we had planned to do it every year."

Unfortunately, fate had another plan for Medha and for all those close to her for the next decade – a decade where Sunita and Junior noticed startling changes in the energetic and lively Medha.

"I salute her and Anup as a couple," said Junior. "They have conducted themselves impeccably. They respect each other and behave with so much grace under pressure."

Sunita echoed Junior's opinion, "I don't think there could be a more dedicated husband than Anup. Amazingly, considering all that they have faced, and still continue to undergo, I have never ever seen any negative emotion in them. Perhaps that is why they have been able to make positive things happen around them."

Sunita may have made that remark unwittingly but medical science has resoundingly agreed with her homespun philosophy.

Indeed, the story of Anup and Medha and the events that led to their meeting and marrying each other, had a fairy-tale feel to it. Forces unknown brought the couple together, "To have and to hold, in sickness and in health, for better or for worse… ."

3

Anup's Chant: Happiness Is Therapeutic

On paper, everything about much-decorated singer Anup Jalota's third marriage spelt "mismatch".

Twice divorced, it was yet another attempt by the *Bhajan Samrat* (Emperor of Devotional Songs, a title bestowed on him) to seek marital bliss. His bride this time was an aristocratic Punjabi, for whom it was a second marriage. Medha's earlier high-profile, traditional wedding to international filmmaker Shekhar Kapur had come apart, and their marriage was formally ended in a court in New Delhi in December 1994.

The singer typified a hearty son-of-the-soil where *bhojan* (food) and bhajan met with aplomb. On the other hand, she, Medha Gujral, former Prime Minister IK Gujral's niece, carried the upper crust air of Delhi around her.

Medha had glimpsed Anup for the first time when her gang of classical music aficionados had gone to hear him at a concert and she had come away with disdain at his heavily compromised semi-classical music. "There he goes," she had smirked along with her friends. "Watch him reach one note and hang on to it till the audience's claps resound through the concert hall." But once Anup and she met as man and woman, Medha's tune changed forever.

December, 2008

At 56, Keluskar Road, Shivaji Park, Mumbai, aptly named 'Mohan Niwas', the abode of a celebrity for whom bhajan singing was serious business, it looked like any normal day. In the garage-morphed-into-an-office, posters of Anup Jalota from his latest film, in the togs of a dacoit, were pasted alongside those of him with a shaven head and benign bliss. Based on the fictional story of a ruthless dacoit who had turned into a Sai Baba devotee, Anup was acting in and producing this film. Popular film star Jackie Shroff, emitting suitable saintliness as Baba, looked down from the same wall. (A couple of years later, Anup also played Sai Baba in another film.)

There was a chuckle and laughter as India's most recognised bhajan singer vowed, "I am going to keep making many more movies." Whether his mainstream Hindi films sank without a trace or he made ingress into regional cinema, nothing could rob him of his enthusiasm or his confidence – his two constant companions on life's uncharted journey.

An organiser burst in. Anup and his staff greeted him with attentive warmth, dates were confirmed, and yet another show was booked.

His son Aryaman came in. Anup's face softened. "I'm hungry," announced the schoolboy who was still in his uniform. "Give me some money, papa." It was such a routine demand from a school-going kid that if you didn't know the truth, you would have taken it as just another blissful day in a regular family.

The truth, however, was heart-achingly the converse.

The voice that could belt out three non-stop hours of traditional Indian songs without a drop in the lung power, broke uncharacteristically as Anup averred in a stage whisper, "This marriage has to survive. I need my wife, my son needs her. Aryaman has hardly known his mother; we both need Medha in our lives."

That December in 2008, Anup had just flown down from New York to Mumbai, after spending six, intensely crucial weeks with his wife in a hospital bed. He was torn between wanting to be beside son Aryaman and wife Medha, the two people who mattered most to him but who were in two different continents. Aryaman went to school in Mumbai and Medha, the wife he wouldn't let go of, was once again battling for life in a New York hospital.

The New York-Mumbai flight plan was one that Anup knew by heart. Seven years ago, he had flown the same route for two unrelenting years when his wife had almost lost the battle for life but had combatted it victoriously. After a seven-year spell of sunshine that had flown by with great speed, Anup was back to flying the New York-Mumbai route, with menacing clouds threatening to envelope his star-crossed love story once again.

Did life deal a fair hand to this man who had spent every working hour, indeed made a career out of singing the full-throated praise of the Lord in all his glorious avatars?

Was there justice when his hard-earned marital bliss was hit by life-threatening turbulence?

The two failed marriages, prior to his finding the perfect partner in Medha, had been well-reported in the '80s when Anup was a bright-eyed new entrant on Mumbai's bustling music horizon. The young romantic had fallen head over heels in love with a spunky music student, a Gujarati girl called Sonali Sheth but when parental disapproval followed, Anup had acquiesced and got engaged to a girl from his own Punjabi community.

"I was seeing Sonali," reminisced the bhajan singer whose chequered love life had nary a closed chapter, "when my parents arranged my marriage with another girl. But *grahon ne,* the planets played such a game that it was in my destiny to marry Sonali. One week before my marriage, I met Sonali again. I saw her and realised that I was still in love with her. We ran away and got married the next day."

And his bride ran away from him the very next year.

"*Grahon ne*," he repeated the reference to astronomy, "the planets have played all kinds of games with me. The planet which rules my marital life is terribly notorious. It has given me a lot of grief." He wryly brought an element of sardonic humour into a situation potent with heartbreak. If Anup's marriage to Sonali defied family, the screechy breakup cocked a snook at societal conventions. His marriage not only broke up, it witnessed Sonali running away with his own accompanist, his *tabalchi* (tabla player), an unknown but talented romantic called Roopkumar Rathod.

'*Tujhme rab dikhta hai, yaaran main kya karoon*,' sang Roopkumar soulfully for Shah Rukh Khan in the 2008 blockbuster Hindi film, *Rab Ne Bana Di Jodi*. The lyrics, sung by a besotted lover to his woman, roughly translated into, 'I glimpse the Almighty in you, I can't help myself.' Steeped in romance, the song exemplified the tabalchi-turned-singer's real life fascination for his woman as Roopkumar and Sonali Rathod soon settled down as a celebrity couple with a rich cultural identity of their own.

But that kind of 'happily ever after' ending was denied to Anup, the husband Sonali had left behind. After Sonali, Anup had bowed down to his parents' wishes once again and agreed to an arranged marriage. His parents had fixed up a match between him and Bina, a Kutchi Bhatia, handpicked by them. Grand invitation cards had gone out from the jubilant Jalota clan to celebrate the return of the prodigal to the fold.

The arranged marriage at a five-star hotel was everything a traditional family would have wanted for their son. But it turned out to be far from an ideal match as Bina couldn't settle down comfortably with the Jalotas. Characteristically, Anup never really spoke up in any interview about what went wrong with this marriage. He wouldn't go beyond saying that Bina didn't get along with the family. Whatever the reason, the outcome was that Anup had to once again face the familiar routine of divorce lawyers and family courts.

A second round of matrimonial disaster would have found most celebrities scurrying into a private corner. But Anup was stoic enough to face the media and accept that his second marriage too, had failed.

"I have been told by a soothsayer," he would tell friends in the media, "that my horoscope does not show a happy marriage till the age of 42, after which I will meet the right girl and know marital bliss." That ray of optimism energised him as he went on to win professional accolades and become the uncrowned Bhajan Samrat.

"Anup is very pragmatic," saluted singer Talat Aziz whose friendship with Anup dated back to their days in Colaba, Mumbai, when both of them were struggling for a place in the sun. Talat had closely watched Anup's many relationships blossom and tumble.

"Actually he is a lot like his father, the late Shri Purushottam Das Jalota. His father was also an amazing gentleman. When he was 80-plus and had problems walking, he would still make it a point to go over to Anup's place and teach his disciples. He always equated me with Hyderabad and, over lunch he once said to me, 'I have never eaten Hyderabadi *biryani* (Indian dish made with highly seasoned rice and meat or vegetables).' So Bina, my wife, made it and sent it to him. He was jovial, fond of good food and he loved mutton biryani.

"Anup has that same *joie de vivre*, whatever the situation. Even when we went over to meet Anup after his father's funeral, there was sadness but no dramatic mourning. On the contrary, he found solace in the fact that his father had gone the way he had lived. His father had suffered a stroke a week before he passed away and he disliked being dependent on anyone. He died soon after. He lived life on his terms, he also died on his own terms. So when we met Anup, he chose to talk about all that instead of getting morbid."

"Anup is a man of great resilience," observed 62-year-old Mumbai-based, freelance journalist, Jyothi Venkatesh who had interviewed the singer at every turn of his life. "He has the mental fibre to overcome any and every kind of crisis. I have met him on various occasions, be it the testing times when his wife Sonali walked out on him to marry Roopkumar Rathod, or the harrowing period when he had to opt for a divorce from his second wife Bina.

"What I have consistently liked about Anup is the fact that however painful the situation, he has never talked against any of his wives, though he may not be godly enough to continue to be good friends with them. Whenever I tried to make him talk about his marriages after they ended, Anup always evaded my question with a '*Wohi hota hai jo manzoor-e-khuda hota hai*', a karmic 'What the gods will, will prevail' kind of acceptance."

Anup met Medha in 1994.

"Our meeting was a beautiful story," Anup smiled beatifically, as he narrated how he had met and wooed Wife No 3. Neelam, wife of late actor Joy Mukherjee, played Cupid.

"Joy Mukherjee and his wife, Neelam were good friends of mine. One evening, Neelam had come over and after dinner we were chatting when she told me that she went for regular walks with Medha, Shekhar Kapur's wife. I said, 'Oh, I also know her, she had come over to my place one day with Pandit Jasraj's group. How is she?' Neelam mentioned to me that Medha was single now. And instantly something inexplicable happened, *ghanti baj gayi,* a bell went off within me, something fell into place. I asked Neelam for Medha's number and at 11 that night. I called her up. Medha sounded angry. She must have thought, 'Who does this guy think he is, calling me up at night like this?' I told her that Neelam had come over for dinner and then out of the blue, I asked her, 'Will you come for lunch tomorrow?' She heard that, grew angrier and demanded why on earth she should do that. I said, 'Just like that, for no particular reason.'

"In the morning, I called her up again and said, 'Coming, aren't you?' And she agreed! I sent her the car, she arrived around 1 pm, I received her at the lift and took her to my music room. We talked for the next two-and-a-half hours. I didn't give her lunch. We just talked and talked and at 3.30 pm I proposed to her. That must have convinced her that I was a complete lunatic."

It was rather dramatic too. "Just as I proposed to her, there was a thunderstorm and heavy winds, the windows were rattling and there was a rumbling sound. The first monsoon rain was lashing Mumbai. I told her, 'See, even nature is with us. You can't say no.' She said, 'Let me think, *khaana toh khilao,* where's my lunch?'" Anup wisecracked, "I had kept her starving, so that she would be too weak to resist my proposal.

"She left after lunch. I began to call her up frequently but in vain. She must have checked up on me. My reputation in the marriage market was very bad and some fellow singers had also delighted in maligning me.

"Medha kept getting negative feedback from everywhere about me but she later said that it puzzled her because personally, she didn't get any wrong vibes from me.

"15 days later, I phoned her from Kolkata and asked her, 'What have you decided?' To my utter delight, she said, 'Yes.' I remember I burst into tears, I cried like a baby. After my programme, I came back to Mumbai and from the airport went straight to Medha's house in Versova. I put her in my car, brought her home and introduced her to my parents as their new daughter-in-law. We had a meal together before I went to drop her off at her place. After that I didn't return to my house for several months. In fact, I returned home only after one year."

Moving into her apartment was as natural and uncomplicated as singing an effortless bhajan. Anup Jalota nodded in agreement, "When Medha accepts someone, she goes the whole hog. She accepts him wholeheartedly with no-holds-barred."

It didn't even occur to him that as the Bhajan Samrat, he had a conventional image to live up to. Anup Jalota strongly believed, "My listeners form their own image of what I must be like, based purely on the fact that I sing bhajans. But I am not a conventional man. I have never liked smoking but I drink openly at parties. I eat non-vegetarian food. When I moved in with Medha, I told her, 'You have accepted me wholeheartedly today. So why should you stay alone anymore? We are together from now on.'"

He added gratefully, "Medha is extremely generous. Once we got together, she gave me carte blanche to do anything I wanted for my family. She told me right from the beginning,

'I'll never come in the way if you ever want to do anything for anybody in your family.' And she hasn't, to this day. We don't stop each other from helping anybody."

The Anup-Medha union was so complete, neither let the past cloud the present bliss.

"Her past didn't bother me one little bit," he frowned at the insinuation that it could be any other way. "If she was married earlier and had people in her life before me, I had a past too. I knew everything about her and I told her everything about me. We wanted to live our lives honestly."

It didn't seem to matter to the besotted suitor that Medha may also never be able to conceive. One of the first problems that had cropped up in Medha's marriage to Shekhar was that her tubes were found blocked. Anup knew about it when he moved in with her with honourable intentions.

"There was a problem," he accepted. "She told me that she would need a surgical procedure if we wanted a baby. Her tubes were blocked, so she couldn't conceive. I told her, 'Just be happy, we'll think about it when the time comes.' But I made her so happy that her tubes opened up naturally. She was so surprised when she discovered she was pregnant! But the fact is, I gave her so much happiness, it was not a miracle, it was a cure, a treatment. Being happy is therapeutic. Everything begins to function normally, the tubes open up; your mind, your body, your whole being responds to happiness."

That feeling of bliss had to culminate at the altar and it did, with characteristic unconventionality. No frills, no fuss.

Anup recalled the simplicity of the occasion. "We were in London when I asked her one night, 'Do you want to get married?' She said, 'Yes.' We got married the next morning.

Only three of us, Medha, Rita and I were present. Rita, who organised my shows, looked for a temple and that was it. We had no reception, nothing at all."

But celebrations went on, non-stop.

Watching from the sidelines, Jyothi Venkatesh reported, "Medha helped restore Anup's faith in life; he had begun to lose faith in the institution of marriage. Ever since she came into his life, year after year, Medha has made it a point to celebrate Anup's birthday, come rain or sunshine."

Close friend and fellow-singer Talat Aziz shared the same opinion as he spoke about Anup's birthday celebrations in July, 2008. "Singer Richa Sharma, Anup and I sang at the party. I was in one of my zany, fun moods. Medha was extremely unwell at that time but she danced with all of us. The next day she sent me a text message that said, 'You should always be in such a fun mood. I liked you in that mood and all the ladies went gaga over you.'" And Talat responded with a gallant, "I don't care about the others. I was only bothered about one charmer, you!"

Jyothi Venkatesh pointed out with the perceptive nose of a reporter, "Strangely, Anup shares July 29, his birthday with actor Sanjay Dutt whose personal life has followed a similar trajectory. Sanjay lost his first girlfriend when he chose drugs over her. Then he floundered after he lost his first wife Richa Sharma to cancer and his second wife Rhea Pillai to Leander Paes till Manyaata brought stability into his life. In much the same way, Anup lost his way till Medha gave him stability."

Anup and Medha as a couple had one common love: "We simply loved throwing parties," said Anup. The birth of their son, Aryaman, was another reason to party. On that occasion, they got renowned classical music vocalist Pandit Jasraj to sing and bless their family in their spacious terrace apartment. "It was only after Medha's health began to deteriorate that there were restrictions," the voice dropped. "Otherwise, in this house there was perpetual *hungama,* happy chaos!"

Hungama and laughter which were soon replaced by hospitals and doctors.

Son Aryaman was barely four years old when Medha collapsed with a rare heart condition that was probably congenital. Hospitals, doctors, frantic stints in American hospitals, an open-heart surgery and chilling verdicts followed. She was sinking, as were their combined finances. As Anup succinctly put it, "The cost of keeping her alive has been much more than what I have earned in my entire career."

A heart transplant in the nick of time brought Medha back from the brink of death. The parties resumed after her return. Anup's 50th birthday was a lavish affair and six years of pure happiness prevailed at Mohan Niwas.

As 2007 came to a close, alarm bells suddenly began to ring again. This time it was the kidneys.

By April 2008, Medha was on dialysis three times a week. "But the other four days of the week are mine to live as I please," she cheerfully announced, at a party thrown by NDTV editor, Abhigyan Prakash. She said it with a bland acceptance sans dramatics. That was a marked feature everywhere – whether at their Shivaji Park residence or in her mother, Dr Vimla Gujral's sprawling Delhi bungalow, whether it was Medha herself, or her son or her siblings, there was a stoic dignity, remarkably free of hysteria.

"I'm living on borrowed time, I know that," Medha said in mid-2008. "I'm now waiting for a donor for a kidney transplant for which I have to go back to the US."

Which would have made Medha an extremely rare, multi-organ transplant patient, delicately poised between life and death.

2008 ended with Medha being rushed to New York where her heartiness evaporated as death stared her in the face again. Through it all, Anup maintained his she'll-pull-through rhetoric, almost planting an auto suggestion in his wife. 2009 dawned with her still critical but out of intensive care and on a flight back to Mumbai.

What gave Medha the courage to remain so calm and blasphemously lively, in the face of death?

What made the family rally around and never dwell on the inevitable? What was the force that kept the entire household running normally when others would have broken down and turned the atmosphere sombre and tense? What drove a man to keep bringing his wife back from the jaws of death, again and again?

"Medha is an iron lady," the fond husband paid his tribute. "No one can take so much and still smile. No one can be ready for the next bout but she is always prepared for it. She knows that her medical issues are a never-ending problem and that she can never be totally cured. But she also knows that she will always enjoy life and keep the family smiling."

Anup himself never looked like a harassed husband. There was a calm, unyielding strength in him that seemed almost surreal.

He soon disclosed that what saw him through crisis after crisis was indeed, a celestially-bestowed gift from Lord Hanuman, the Hindu God who embodies unflinching loyalty and incalculable reserves of strength.

"When I was seven years old, I gained extra power from God," revealed Anup. "One evening, my father, Purushottamdas Jalotaji was singing at a Hanuman temple in Lucknow. I used to sit behind him and sing along at all his programmes. But on that particular day, I didn't sing even one single line with him. He was puzzled and when he looked behind to see why I was so quiet, he found that all through his two hours of singing, I had been crying. I couldn't sing at all.

"I later explained to my father that I had felt Hanumanji's presence right next to me, I had seen Hanumanji sitting right there in person and that had overwhelmed me. From that day onwards, I have had some extra power, there is an unbelievable strength in me.

"Strangely, from that day onwards, I also lost the quality of *krodh*, of anger, rage. I never get angry and it has been like this since the age of seven. I never lose my temper or fight with anybody. In fact, this has been the biggest complaint all my ex-wives have had against me – that this man never gets angry," he chuckled.

"The absence of anger," he philosophised, "gives me so much *shanti,* peace. When anger is absent, it doubles your energy because anger burns up your energy negatively."

In the place of anger was a stubborn refusal to throw up his hands in despair, however major the crisis before him.

"After all my bad marriages, I really want this marriage to survive and it will," he was obstinately positive about it. "I genuinely love Medha. She is the mother of my child. She is a part of my life in every way and we are very attached to each other. This is a marriage that has worked wonderfully. There has been only a medical problem clouding our happiness."

However dismissive he was about it, the medical problem must surely have come in the way of having a normal husband-wife relationship? Anup never saw it from that perspective.

"No, it does not," he emphatically refuted the thought. "In the hospital I sleep next to her. At home, we share the same room. Okay, there are a few restrictions, a few problems because of which physical intimacy is sometimes restricted. But according to me, we do more than other couples. I am so romantic with her, even in public I hold her hand, sometimes I sing for her in front of other people. I think all this means more than physical intimacy. And Medha enjoys it."

Painter and art curator Bina Aziz, wife of Talat Aziz, actually witnessed it. "One day we had gone to see Medha after dialysis. Normally she loses her stamina after the procedure. Anup was there just holding her hand, smiling, saying nothing. I could see that it was very important for her, it keeps her going."

It was admirable for any man to romance his ailing wife. But didn't Anup ever feel like straying?

"I will never have an extra-marital affair," Anup declared with Bheeshma-like resolve. (Bheeshma in the Indian epic Mahabharat, took a vow of celibacy that he followed till his death at a ripe old age.) "Friendship yes, affair, never. I have male and female students around me. It doesn't mean that because I have their moral and emotional support, I will have an affair with any of them.

"People don't exactly advise me to move on but they do tell me that no husband will do so much for his wife. My answer to that is, if a husband doesn't do it, who will? In our *shastras*, our holy books, it is said that a husband and wife are each other's *ardhangini*, two parts of one body. It means half her body is mine. So why won't I look after my own body, go all out to do my best for it? I don't do it because I have to. I do it with love, with awareness, with total acceptance. I keep selling off my properties, my cars. I bought a Mercedes twice, sold it both times.

"What it has cost me is easily, in one line, more than what I have earned in my life. Everybody came forward to help me because I never had so much money. Even Medha's ex-husband, Shekhar Kapur helped us out. Of course I returned every rupee to everyone. The money going out is more than I earn but it doesn't rattle me or give me sleepless nights. The money comes when it has to. I am still one of the top singers of this country, people come to me regularly for shows and I get good money. All the money I collect goes to Mr Hospital.

"I am never insecure about money. I love making money but I don't attach importance to holding on to it. I don't show my problems to anybody because I know I have the capacity to overcome them on my own. I show only my happiness to people, not my sorrows."

Talat vouched for that impressive quality in his friend. "I have always known Anup to be cheerful, perpetually smiling and very positive. You can see his carefree attitude even when he's singing live, nothing fazes him. Hats off to him, he's never shown any kind of slump in his spirits. When his personal relationships didn't work out, somewhere inside him, he must have felt bad but he always had that rare ability to bounce back. He must be going through his share of stress and problems but he doesn't ever show it."

Anup dissected his approach to life's many impossible demands and reiterated, "Duties are never a burden and I have enjoyed performing them in life. They have to be done with full faith. I am not a religious person but I do things religiously.

"We have never created a sombre atmosphere at home, we have never let Aryaman see how critical the situation sometimes is."

It almost sounded like Anup was in denial when he suddenly remarked, "Medha is so fond of the hills, the raw, untouched hills. She is not the sort who wants to go to Dubai for its large shopping malls. I used to take her twice a year to places like Himachal. When she returns this time, I will take her to Khandala. On alternate days, when there is no dialysis, I will take her to places where she gets her happiness. Whatever is left of life, we will spend it making each moment count."

The point was, how much of her life was left for her to enjoy? In Anup's own words, "She had one heart transplant seven years ago. Now, because of the heavy medication, her kidneys are gone.

"The kidney transplant is not possible until she gains some strength in her body. She is currently too weak for it. I am trying everything that's available to bring her back to health, *kaise bhi theek thaak use leke aaoon.* I know it's tough. It's hard on us emotionally, it's hard on us financially, and it's hard on me professionally too. I give up so many shows when there's a crisis. I have called up organisers and told them, 'Please take your advance back, I'm sorry,' and rushed off whenever a problem has cropped up.

"*Bhagwan sab dekh raha hai.* God is watching everything. I'm sure she'll be fine. He has sent us unconditional support from so many people. Apart from her family, there are two couples to whom we are heavily indebted for all their help and support in New York. Ashok and Gargi Bajaj in New Jersey and my cousin Radhika and her husband Mridul Tandon. They have gone out of their way to help us, even reaching the hospital at 5 am when needed. Who does so much for anybody these days? When Medha had her heart transplant in New York, my sister Anita and her husband Raje moved into our house in Mumbai and took care of Aryaman. So many have pitched in and helped. These people gave us their precious time. We can't ever forget our support systems."

One of these invaluable "support systems", Anup's Mumbai-based sister, Anita Raje never let little Aryaman feel that anything was amiss. That was the unmistakable Indian trait of going out of one's way to help but looking at it simply as something that must be done for one's family.

"We are family and it's our duty," said Anita. "We haven't done anything out of the way, these things are done in any family."

Husband Raje chimed in, "As long as Medha comes back safely, nothing else really matters."

Echoing Anup's optimism, Anita endorsed, "She will come back cured, and she will be fine, it's our *vishwas* (belief)."

What Anita did was to give Aryaman a normal home to come back to after school. "We never leave Aryaman alone. We ensure that," she explained. "We also keep the house as normal as possible, so Aryaman doesn't feel that there's a crisis happening. Aryaman is a son of our family."

It was this traditional Indian family support that made Anup veto all attempts by Medha's family to send Aryaman to a boarding school. "Boarding is for children who need to be disciplined. My son is fine, he's happy in this atmosphere," said Anup firmly. "We have good staff; everybody keeps an eye on him. He gets the food he wants and we have family here. He's busy with school on weekdays and he spends his weekends with his cousins. I'm against sending him to boarding. I won't let anybody send him to boarding school," he promised Aryaman.

And he promised to bring back his wife alive, once again. Meanwhile, it was apparent that a healthy, full-bodied married life had been denied to him once again and Anup accepted it with calm resignation. "What has happened to this marriage is proof that I can never have a regular, trouble-free marriage," he remarked.

"*Meri kundli ke ek ghar mein bahut dushman baithe hain*. There's something in my horoscope that's inimical to me. I am sure about it now. Otherwise, a person like me who has never troubled anybody should not have to go through all that I have. But if it's God's will that we have to face this crisis, we will. We will make the most of our life together and feast on the happy moments that we spend together. During her heart transplant, we had the best time of our lives. We were living together and having so much fun. It will be the same again, I am sure about that." It was like he had a mantra of his own; his own *The Secret* that had worked before and will work again.

One of the chants was to recall every anxious moment as a happy one. It is a trait that all three – Anup, Medha and Aryaman – share. They talked of the hospital rounds and life in New York the way most others would describe a carefree family holiday.

Anup narrated an amusing anecdote about the time Medha regained consciousness after undergoing the heart transplant.

"The doctors had said that she needed a larger heart than the one she had, so that the other organs could function better with improved blood circulation. She was given a heart double the size of her original one.

"When Medha opened her eyes after the surgery, she saw me and the nurse and the first thing she said was, 'This nurse has looked after me so well, you must give her a hundred dollars.' I told her that these people don't take money; we'll get chocolates or a gift later on. But Medha was adamant that I give her a hundred dollars right then. So I gave it to the nurse and I said to Medha, it's confirmed that you have a larger heart now." When the humour evaporated, emotions surfaced. Anup repeated, "We love each other, we enjoy being together. But yes, life is a little hard. We have to overcome too many problems to be able to enjoy our life together. The price we pay to be together is very high. But it's fine, we can afford it." It was not the money he was referring to but 'afford' as in his immense reserves of strength.

"Through all this, I once again accept that I can never have a smooth marriage," he shook his head. "Medha's heart transplant confirmed beyond doubt that a trouble-free marriage was not in my destiny. When I married Medha, I thought that marital strife was a thing of the past. But we were suddenly hit by her illness."

An illness that has, frustratingly, gone on and on for the larger part of their life together.

"But I have never ever regretted it, not even for a moment," he asserted. "Medha has given me such a beautiful son; it makes up for everything that we have gone through. There is no regret at all and that's why I'm happy. I'm still travelling all over the world and working.

"Besides, Medha has been a wonderful wife. She has a lovely relationship with everybody in my family. She had a fantastic equation with my father." If there was a tiny hiccup, it was, "A little *saas-bahu* (mother-in-law, daughter-in-law) skirmish promoted by Ekta Kapoor!" he laughed, referring to the mother-in-law vs daughter-in-law battles that dominate soaps on Indian television.

Short moments of laughter and smiles eased the tension. But it was omnipresent, always peeping from a short distance away.

"This is Medha's fourth life," Anup counted. "This time when I bring her back, it will be the fourth life we have got from God." It was always 'when I bring her back' and never a doubting 'if'.

"The first time was in Mayo Clinic in Rochester, when she had an open-heart surgery," Anup enumerated the many times death had come visiting and been sent back. "She was sinking, she was going but with a lot of effort she came back from the brink of death. The second time was during her heart transplant. The third time was in Mumbai a few years ago when she had an infection and was at death's door. She was in a terrible state then. This is the fourth, and this time she is in a very critical condition."

It was like running the marathon forever without reaching the finishing point. Wouldn't anybody tire in these circumstances? But at no point did Anup give up the battle.

"Never! I will never call it quits," he was unwavering in his statement. "I'm a fighter. This time, for the first time, Medha herself told me, 'Let me go, I can't take it anymore.' But I said, 'No, we're going to fight it.' She was in great pain and she told me, 'I can't bear it, let me go, stop doing so much for me.' But I said, 'I'm going to bring you back.' And it will happen. Within a month or two, I will bring my beautiful wife back dancing."

He did. In January 2009, Medha touched Chhatrapati Shivaji International Airport in Mumbai, in a wheelchair. Exhausted, frail and too battle-worn to take a step on her own but alive and breathing. Anup Jalota had done it again and brought his wife back from the jaws of death for the fourth time.

The big battle that now faced them was a kidney transplant which was imperative to take Medha off dialysis and give her a whiff of the hearty life that she had been born with.

4

Shekhar Kapur's Robust Bride, Medha

1981, Mumbai

Medha Gujral from Delhi, rechristened Mrs Shekhar Kapur in Mumbai, was wide-eyed.

It was a typical Sunday lunch in poet Kaifi Azmi and his actress-wife Shaukat's Juhu cottage where their vivacious young daughter, Shabana Azmi, lived with her parents.

Shabana, a Hindi film actor who had already garnered great repute for mastery over her craft, took pride in the generous Azmi family table which beckoned friends and guests at any given meal-time. Shabana was wont to describe the bonhomie with the satisfying observation, "There's always extra food cooked at home. Half-a-dozen unexpected guests can always be fed *araam se*, satisfactorily, without any problem."

On Sundays particularly, this welcoming household drew the articulate new film brood, which included filmmakers like Mahesh Bhatt and Vinod Pande, actor Marc Zuber and Shabana's ex-fiancé, Shekhar Kapur with Medha, his pretty young bride from Delhi.

"I was very fascinated by Shabana's house," recalled Medha. "Those days Mahesh Bhatt would come there and Marc Zuber lived across the road in a fascinating house next to Prithvi Theatre. The whole atmosphere was very *mazedcar,* full of fun for me. I was enjoying my marriage with Shekhar, not because of him but in spite of him. I would enjoy meeting these people. I was fascinated by Kaifi Azmi and Shaukat *Aapa* (elder sister) because I hadn't seen people like them in my life before."

The fact that her husband, Shekhar, had once been engaged to Shabana didn't pose a problem to either the new bride or to his former fiancée.

"Shabana's past equation with Shekhar didn't bother me at all," Medha shrugged. "I also had a past and it stood to reason that Shekhar being 10 years older, would have had more of a past than me. Shabana accepted me with real grace. It took her mother, Shaukat *Aapa* a bit of time but eventually she also grew fond of me and I'm still very fond of her."

Nobody at that animated table could have ever predicted that the robust Punjabi girl Shekhar had wed, would one day have one of the most prolonged battles with her life.

The newly-married girl was, on the contrary, positively bursting with health. Medha narrated this amusing bit of conversation with a twinkle in her eye: "We were having lunch at Shabana's place and I was my usual Delhi self, eating away heartily. Suddenly there was silence at the table. Kaifi *Saab*, Shabana, Mahesh Bhatt were all there when Shaukat *Aapa* said, '*Bhai* Shekhar, *tumhari* wife, *mashallah, iska* appetite *toh bahut achcha hai.'* (Shekhar, your wife, God Bless, sure has a hearty appetite.) And I wondered, 'Wow, am I eating too much?'"

There was actually just too much of youthful energy all around Medha to give anybody an inkling of what was to follow in the years to come.

"There was a lot of fun with the Juhu crowd," she recalled. "There was filmmaker Chetan Anand's son, Kunky, Protima Bedi lived next door. Pooja (Bedi), who was a little girl then, would come home from school in Sanawar and say, 'Medha Aunty, see, I baked a cake.' It was a lovely time."

It would, however, be incorrect to say that there was nothing of import even in Medha's childhood to indicate that she would one day be battered by life-threatening illness. In her childhood, the first blip was indeed spotted on the radar. Her early years also explained the unbelievable mental fibre that saw this misleadingly fragile-looking patient combat setback after setback, emotional, physical and spiritual.

5

A Privileged Childhood

1955, New Delhi

Life started comfortably enough on June 25, 1955, in a large, sprawling bungalow on Barakhamba Road in New Delhi. Its residents, the Gujrals, were a respectable, well-placed Delhi family.

On the shoulders of Medha's father, Vijaya Gujral, the only son of this wealthy family, was the responsibility of carrying on a flourishing construction business, an inheritance that his artistic temperament was eminently unsuited for. His wife, Dr Vimla Gujral, a paediatrician by profession, was a rarity – a working woman at a time when only kitchen and kids featured on the daily menu of most other women of her generation.

Medha grew up in this unconventional household, with three feisty siblings cosseting her.

Medha's childhood transported one to a Jane Austen world – a flurry of excitement and emotions provided by a bright, well-spoken quartet of daughters, presided over by indulgent parents, Vijaya and Vimla Gujral.

Vijaya Gujral was a Sanskrit scholar and all his four daughters got traditional Sanskrit names. The eldest daughter, Kushla, got her name because she was just such a happy child. The second, Kirti's name meant fame. Medha stood for brains and intellect while Eeda simply meant prayer, the first verse of the Rig Veda.

Medha, the third in the pecking order, explained, "Kushla Sahgal is eight years older than me. She did architecture and got married into a business family in Chandigarh. There was no scope for a career those days, so she became a socialising housewife. Kirti Parashar studied to be a dietician but worked with Air India for many years. She met her husband, Ashok there. Now both Kushla and Kirti have grandchildren, so my mother has five great grandchildren.

"I was a fairly healthy child and I played a lot of sports," rewound Medha. The only fleeting concern was a murmur in her heart that was heard when she turned 11. "It was a benign murmur and all the investigations revealed nothing worrisome," she expanded. "At one point the doctors had stopped me from playing some games but I was soon back at it.

"I was also dancing in school. I played Draupadi (from the Mahabharat) in a school ballet. Even at the time I met Anupji, I was swimming a lot. I used to live in Versova in Mumbai and go to Sun-n-Sand in Juhu for a swim. I would do 40 laps a day. In fact," she added with a laugh, "one of the reasons why Shekhar liked me was because he felt I was this wholesome Punjabi girl!"

The picture of an active brat, apparently not ill at all, was corroborated by eldest sister Kushla who recalled, "I was aware of the murmur but I was also very young then, busy with school and college. Except for our parents, Medha's illness didn't affect the rest of us. And our parents didn't give us too many details either. Medha was also never ill or in bed. She was doing everything, going to school, playing sports and participating in plays, ballets. Outwardly, she looked normal. The only time mummy would remind us of her illness was when we had a fight with her because she was quite a naughty little thing. Then mummy would say, 'She is not well, let her be.' But of course we didn't let her be," Kushla laughed. "I still fought with her. Since I was so much older than her, I thought I had the right to let her have it."

Since the age of four, Tani (Sandhu) Bhargav and Medha have been really close buddies, notching up a wonderful five-decade friendship between them. Delhi-based Tani too, had the same sort of memories about the murmur that didn't create a flutter, as she put on record, "Medha was taken out of dance class because of the murmur in her heart. As kids we heard it as '*mar-mar* in her heart' which sounded very scary. To me, Medha looked as fit as a fiddle, she could run faster than me, could long-jump better than I did, and her heart condition didn't show up in any way. She swam a lot, she ran a lot, and she and I were always competing to come first. If I jumped high on a pogo stick, she would jump higher. These were pretty strenuous activities. The Indian Army had put up an obstacle course in Delhi and she and I were the only girls who could cross it."

However, the murmur was not so casually dismissed by doctor-mom Vimla. "Medha got a heart murmur very early in life. It was discovered when she was just one year old," disclosed Vimla. "I took her for checkups and the doctors said, 'It's nothing, it will disappear.' But it gradually increased. I showed her to my professor, a cardiologist, and to doctors at the All India Institute of Medical Sciences too. All of them maintained that the murmur was not a major issue. But it kept increasing and around puberty, breathlessness set in. When that continued, I showed her to all the leading doctors in Delhi and they did their best to investigate it.

"However, once she felt a little better, she would again be very active. She was never one to sit and brood. But we were regularly checking on what to do about the murmurs, we kept consulting the best of doctors.

"When she got married to Shekhar, he also came with me for checkups with heart specialists. At that time too, the doctors said it was nothing to worry about. Only when the murmurs kept increasing in 2000, and she fell seriously ill, did the heart problem really surface."

Medha certainly didn't lose any sleep over it. "I was never a sickly child as such. The murmur was just an extra sound in my heart. And nobody connected it to the heart problem I later had."

However, Vimla Gujral didn't dismiss it so easily. She continued to have it investigated. Medha remembered, "Those days there was no echocardiogram in Delhi. The facility was available only in government hospitals like King Edward Memorial (KEM) in Mumbai. I remember going there in my two plaits and them asking, 'Who is the patient?' An echocardiogram is so common these days but I had to go down to Mumbai for it those days. I was only 11 years old, so it was an unpleasant experience." It was also an experience that she had quickly shoved aside as inconsequential since life was too inviting to be menaced by one bothersome detail.

Medha described herself as, "Interested in life, in people. I was an extrovert, a little tomboyish; I used to play cricket and *lattoo* (spinning a top) with the boys in the neighbourhood. I was a happy child."

Indeed, Medha had a privileged childhood and she drew maximum joy out of each and every moment. Blessed with the gift of positive energy, Medha lived life to the fullest, leaving no room for complaints or regrets.

"I had a very happy childhood, it was a very positive atmosphere at home," she affirmed. "There was always something happening, a lot of hustle and bustle, people coming in and going out. Ours used to be the central house for the whole Gujral clan. And because it was spacious, a lot of weddings also took place in our house."

The bungalow burst with so much activity that the question of feeling lonely or neglected never arose, even though her mother was a career woman. "There was never any resentment over having a working mother," Medha said flatly. "She would come home for lunch, travel was so quick those days, and she would be back from work by 4 pm.

"On the days that she couldn't come back early, I used to get into the car after school and fetch her. On those occasions, I would soak in the whole hospital atmosphere. Next to mom's room was the neo-natal clinic. I used to love going and seeing the babies, the hospital smell, everything. Now the hospitals smell differently. They don't use the strong disinfectant Phenyl or whatever to clean the place anymore. So the smell has changed.

"My mother worked for a government hospital for the poor, so the smell of dust and sweat was predominant. It was frequented by very poor people who, after getting cured, would send letters to my mother saying, 'You are God.' They came from remote villages and her speciality was polio. She and the department would rehabilitate children who were polio-afflicted. They also started going to the slums to get children vaccinated.

"My mother was into a lot of genuine social work. After my father's death, she formed a Vijaya Gujral Foundation which adopted a village for slum rehabilitation. She opened a primary school there, a primary health centre and a centre for women for stitching. All of us contributed to it. It was run by all four of us sisters pitching in with our money.

"Every year on September 16, my father's birth anniversary, my mother would organise a function for Bicodep, the name of the project. One year, we had a well dug for each of the five sectors of Bicodep. I gave some money for planting trees because I found their place so barren and dry. Whatever money we had, we gave to the Foundation and my mother would direct its flow. When she was older and couldn't handle it anymore, she got the local Rotary Club involved in it."

All her life, Medha knew her mother to be an active working woman.

"Yes," said Vimla, 83 years old in 2008. "I had a career when my children were born. So I was always working and simultaneously looking after them. I did honorary work at first. I would go in the morning for two-three hours and come back by lunchtime."

Vimla's story reflected the kind of genes she passed on to her daughters – there was a distinct unconventionality and sharp intelligence visible in all her children.

The family Vimla was born in and the one she got married into were crammed with businessmen. Yet, she qualified as a professional because her father, Amolak Ram Sarin, was very keen that everybody, especially all the girls, should study. "My eldest sister went into teaching. I took the premedical. At that time only three people from Punjab, two Muslims and one Hindu would be taken into Lady Hardinge College. I was one of the three to be selected.

"It was very rare in our time for girls to study and work," she accepted. "But it was okay for us because my family was all for it. In my fourth year at Lady Hardinge, I got married. At that time I had to take special permission to leave boarding. After my marriage, I started going to college from home."

Her husband, Vijaya Gujral, had lost his father when he was barely six years old. So Vimla went into a house that was presided over by her husband's grandfather. "At the time of my marriage, my husband was not keen that I continue studying but his grandfather was keen that I complete the medical course. My grandfather-in-law wanted me to study and do honorary work. So I started with the Arya Samaj (Hindu sect that does not believe in idol worship) and then took on an honorary job at Lady Hardinge."

An Arya Samaji who believed in the uplift of women, there was an interesting reason for the canny old man to keep young Vimla out of the house. Two women, his own wife and his son's widow, were already running the bungalow. So, when his grandson's wife, Vimla, stepped in, she had a mother-in-law and a grandmother-in-law to contend with. The smart old man foresaw a battle *royale* in the house if this young daughter-in-law also joined the fray and therefore encouraged her to study and work outside the house.

The Arya Samaj philosophy was so well adhered to in her childhood bungalow that Medha commented, "Today, I have a small temple in my house with Anupji but I'm sure in 17, Barakhamba Road, it would never have been allowed."

Feminism was still a faraway concept in Indian society when Dr Vimla Gujral successfully balanced a demanding career with a normal household. Vimla credited it to the joint family. "My mother-in-law, grandfather-in-law, his wife and a maid were all there. Also, my house was very near the hospital. My children went to Modern School which was also close by. When they went to school, I would go to the hospital.

"I could even do my post-graduation," she pointed out. "I did my doctorate in paediatrics in Delhi and got my Diploma in Child Health, DCH, from London. I went abroad for one year, did my DCH and post-graduation. I was given a scholarship and a special fellowship for rehabilitation to Copenhagen. The day my husband died, I got promoted to Professor, Paediatrics. Then I had to start attending work full-time."

That was the point when Vimla wanted to wind up her career and be with her daughters. But the children wouldn't hear of it. "Yes," she acknowledged. "I continued working and finished my professorship. Everybody, especially the girls, supported me."

Her four girls provided the bereaved young widow the support system to keep going. If Vimla was ever wistful about having a string of daughters and no son, it was only when other people pointed it out to her. While she accepted that having a son might have been nice only as a change, she was staunchly loyal to her brood as she disarmingly stated, "I have enjoyed having each of my girls."

Vimla Gujral wouldn't dream of calling any of her girls a tomboy but she accepted that Medha was more energetic than the others. "She used to take part in everything. In school too, wherever there was any *kami* (shortfall), she would fill in. Whether it was dramatics or dance, she was good at everything. She was an all-rounder."

If Medha was the perky one, eager to dabble in everything that life had to offer, she was also the pesky one who got on her eldest sister, Kushla's nerves and bullied Eeda, the youngest one. Kirti, who bears a stark resemblance to Medha, however, has quite the opposite personality. Always the quiet observer, she ruffled no feathers and remained unflappable too.

"Maybe because Medha and I were both so similar, we always had clashes," said Kushla, with a big smile that childhood remembrances invariably bring to a person. "It went on till 1965 when mummy went to Denmark on a WHO fellowship. She told me before leaving, 'You are the eldest, so you will have to look after all of them.' That was when Medha and I got really close. Until then, she made sure she irritated me and I made sure that I got irritated.

"There were minor clashes. When I would teach her Maths, which she was always bad at, she would irritate me by saying, 'This is not the method we have been taught.' There are always three or four different methods to solve every problem. Every method I tried to teach her was 'not it' till I would get irritated."

Medha certainly knew how to irk Kushla. She would burst into a KL Saigal number that described an elephant's walk, "*Rum-jhum, rum-jhum, chaal tihari, kahe bhaiy, Iravat matwari...*" and bang-on, Kushla would want to strangle her.

"She would needle me over little things and I would want to hit her. We used to run round and round the drawing room and she would say, *'Moti, pakad nahin sakti'* (you can't catch me, fatso), and stuff like that. I have been plump ever since I was 12 or 13 years old while Medha was always slim. So there were always these little sibling skirmishes which one purposely indulges in. But otherwise there was never any major quarrel between us."

It was during her mother's absence that Medha reached puberty and it was Kushla who stepped in to make her understand what was happening to her young body. Until then, all Medha had known was that there was one taboo drawer at home used by her two older sisters who kept something in it. But she was never allowed to open and peep into it.

That one incident changed Medha's equation with Kushla forever.

On the other hand, Eeda Chopra, the youngest of the four, shuddered, "Medha was a bully. We used to share a room till I was 16 and she was 21. It was only when Kirti got married that I got a room of my own. Medha and Tani have been friends forever. So whenever they wanted their own time and I was around, they would go, 'Bye Eeda, bye.' Even now when they meet, if they want to irritate me, they still say, 'Bye, Eeda, bye!'"

The fun and laughter in a house full of spirited young girls got its first real jolt in 1974 when the benign presence of their father, Vijaya Gujral, was suddenly removed from the picture-perfect family portrait.

The early death of the father Medha was so close to – he was the person she had rushed to when she had her first big college romance – was perhaps the first cloud in her clear blue sky. However, her mother had already experienced grief and pain years ago, when one of her daughters, Vibha, had succumbed to cirrhosis of the liver at the tender age of 11.

Close family friend Tani could not help but feel that early deaths in the family had made a deep impact on the Gujrals. "I have always felt that the deaths affected the family a lot," she reflected. "I feel that the death of Medha's sister, Vibha, put a cold little fist around everyone's heart. Then Uncle (Medha's father) died young and even though Aunty (Vimla) was a doctor, nothing could be done to save him. In retrospect, I wonder if these two deaths had some kind of connection with Medha's cardiomyopathy." Restrictive cardiomyopathy was the heart disease which took Medha to the brink of death in 2000.

Medha didn't have any memory of Vibha's death. "Vibha *Didi* (elder sister) died of a congenital liver problem. I was barely three or four years old when she died, so I don't remember her at all. I was born in 1955, she died in '59."

For her mother though, it was a major heartbreak. "It happened so suddenly," recalled Vimla. "Vibha got hepatitis and very high fever, then cirrhosis. It took a few months for her to pass away but being a doctor, I knew what was happening. We showed her to the best of specialists here, had her blood tested abroad. I knew it was serious and it was traumatic for me."

But not for Medha.

Too young to be affected by her sister's death, it was the death of her father on May 8, 1974 that dealt her the killer blow. She later wondered if it was the harbinger of her own heart condition. Clearly, her father's presence and absence had made a deep impression on Medha.

He had a big hand in shaping Medha's interests, especially in inculcating a taste for the fine arts. Vijaya Gujral was in the construction business. "So we were actually quite a typical Punjabi business family," Medha pertly remembered. But the major flaw in the diamond was that Vijaya had a classic distaste for his inheritance – he had zero interest in the family business.

Medha drew a vivid picture of a warm and wonderful man who would have rather read books, tinkered with cars or sneaked off at midnight for a music concert and discussed the intricacies of a raga than expended energy on a business deal.

In Medha's words, "My father had a very literary background. He never went to school, tutors would come home. He was good at Sanskrit and Psychology. He read a lot, I used to read most of his books, whether it was John Steinbeck or Bachchan."

Vijaya Gujral handed to Medha not a head for figures but a heart that came alive with dance and song. He could spend hours with his music and the Gujral house reverberated with the sound of ragas that wafted out of his vast collection of EPs and LPs. His ancient record player later made way for huge German Grundig tapes but classical music remained a constant love.

Medha stated, "My father had ingrained a lot of things in me like reading, philosophy and classical music. I was a little girl when the Shankar Lal Festival would take place across the road in my school. He would wake me up at midnight and say, 'Aamir Khansaab is singing raga *malkauns* (late-night pentatonic raga belonging to the Shaivait musical school), let's go and hear him.' I would trot across with him in my night suit and I would lie down there while he would listen to music. Thus, there was music in me right from the beginning."

Medha also recalled that her father had a heart problem from an early age. "He was a smoker and a drinker. He would hide and smoke. We had this huge old house with a driveway all around it. You had to enter from a gate; there was a garden, porch, house and then a back garden. From every toilet there was an exit door at the back for the *jamadaar* (scavenger) to go in and clean it without entering the main house. My father would go into a toilet, vanish through the back door, smoke and return to the house. He destroyed his health because of that.

"My father probably died of the same problem that I had with my original heart. Those days, there was no such diagnosis and there was no cure for it. There was no availability of a transplant either. My father had a couple of heart attacks but he always came back home. Strangely, when he passed away, he had gone in for a hernia operation and he didn't come out of it alive. By then, he had kind of lost the will to live. He had a lot of work-related problems; he wasn't cut out for business."

An inescapable turn of events had landed Medha's artistically-inclined father in an alien world of numbers and accounts books. He was the only son of Vidyadhar Gujral who in turn had been the only son of Lala Gyanchandji. It was not easy for Vijaya Gujral to play a winning hand with the cards dealt out to him as the scion of that business stock.

Poignantly tracing the family tree, Medha noted, "As Arya Samajis, they used to live according to the Vedas. When my father's father, Vidyadhar Gujral, took over the business, my great grandfather, Lala Gyanchandji, left Delhi and went to Haridwar to live an ascetic life. He had taken *vanaprastha* (retreat into the forest) and given up worldly pleasures. But my grandfather died when my father was only six years old and so, my great grandfather had to come back to Delhi to complete his (dead) son's duties. He still lived like a hermit, withdrawn, away from his wife but he carried on the business till my father grew up. So my father was pushed into a business which didn't suit his temperament."

Alas! Medha's father had no choice but to reluctantly don the mantle of a businessman and relieve his ageing grandfather of his responsibilities. When Vijaya Gujral played with his life by continuing to smoke despite an acute heart problem, it was as if he had made a secret death wish. The wish was granted to him early, leaving his wife a widow before she had even reached menopause.

"My husband was a heavy smoker, right from the beginning," recalled Vimla who lost him when she was only 48 years old.

"He was a smoker from his college days. I was 18 or 19 and he was only 21 when we got married. He continued smoking even after a heart attack. He was strictly forbidden to but he smoked till the end."

In the '60s, when television arrived in India, a black-and-white TV set was brought into the Gujral bungalow. In a long room where the set was installed, everybody would gather in the evenings, including the servants and their kids, to watch TV. It was etched in Medha's memory that her dad would make sure he stood right at the back where he couldn't be spotted by anybody. When she would turn back, Medha would see Vijaya quickly take a puff from his cigarette, nursing a drink in the other hand. Medha's mother explained, "My husband never smoked in front of his grandfather. He always obeyed him, went to the Arya Samaj and did everything that was expected of him."

It killed his spirit but Vijaya played his part of the dutiful son even though his own passions lay far away from the family business. His wife described him as, "Very literary, very intelligent, very good with his hands; he could even make my medical instruments. But he had to take over the business from his grandfather and he was not cut out for it. He preferred to read, the girls picked up that habit from him. Medha's interest in music also came from him."

Family friend Tani had her own special remembrance of "Uncle". To this day, she has a pair of chairs that Medha's father had made with his own hands. She had found them lying broken on the terrace with pigeon droppings on them. She instantly recognised them from her childhood days, took home two that could be salvaged from a set of six, and had them refurbished.

"They were made of fabulous Burmese teak," explained Tani. "They only needed to be restrung and looked after well. One day, I asked Aunty to sit on them and she couldn't believe that they were the same chairs.

"Uncle was someone who really worked magic with his hands. Whether it was restoring cars which was a passion with him, or making furniture, he was hands on.

"He was a very soft-spoken man, the only son in a business family but with no interest in business. None whatsoever," she emphasised. It was heartrending that Vijaya's complete lack of interest in business was obvious even to his children and their friends.

Tani recalled that Vijaya Gujral was always at home and eternally doing something admirably creative. A man with deep and diverse interests, he was also good at photography and had a beautiful collection of black-and-white pictures.

"He once shot a picture of mine which made me look glamorous even as a kid. He would wait, let us talk, make us feel comfortable and then suddenly say, 'It's done, you can go now,'" recalled Tani, lovingly.

Medha also fondly remembered her artistic parent as a man who had, "Crazy friends like Vekki (Vivek) Uncle who had a beard and a cigar all the time. He also had no interest in his family business and left it very soon. Vekki Uncle went to the Himalayas and stayed in Binsar (in Uttarkhand, near Almora) in an orchard. These were the kind of friends my father had, far removed from the business world.

"My uncle, Inder Gujral who later became the Prime Minister of India, was in and out of our house. He was beginning to get involved in politics, so all the sessions used to be held in the office part of our house. Inder Gujral was my father's first cousin. After Partition when he and his brother, Satish Gujral, came to India as refugees, they were given some property but no money to run anything. Our family had been in Delhi for four generations, so my father could help them a little, even financially. For a while, Inder Uncle's office also used to be in our house and he was very close to my father.

"Those were the coffee-house days when they would all gather in a coffee house in Connaught Place and discuss politics. Inder Uncle was influenced by Jawaharlal Nehru and joined the Congress.

"So I grew up in an atmosphere of music, politics and business."

It was an ideal childhood and Medha eagerly trod the creative avenues that were opened out to her. But the ecstasy was snuffed out when Vijaya Gujral died all of a sudden. Medha was not even 19 years old then and the unexpected punch staggered her. But her doctor-mother had feared for long that the end was around the corner.

"Being a doctor, my mother knew that my father's end would come sooner than expected because after a heart attack, he was still smoking a lot," said Medha. "She couldn't have handled his passing away if she didn't have a job. After he died, she didn't want to but we pushed her to go back to her career. She got promoted as Professor of Paediatrics, something that my father had always wanted for her."

Her professional commitments were therapeutic for Vimla. She cheered up, began to travel a lot and even visited Japan with her friends.

In her childhood, when Medha's own heart had begun to sound not quite right and the murmurs were noticed, her father had been alive and he had his own way of reassuring her about it.

"He used to say, if there is a need for it, we will both go abroad and get our hearts treated," Medha remembered. "However, at that time, there was no need for me to go for treatment while his heart had already gone bad. I now tend to think that my problem could have been genetic because one of my sisters also has a heart problem, slightly different from mine. My grandfather also died young."

Cardiologist and close family friend, Dr Alok Chopra was inclined to go with Medha's line of thought, though Vimla would not buy her daughter's presumption. "My husband did have a heart attack but I can't say if it was genetic," she debated, pointing out, "His grandfather lived to his eighties. And my father-in-law may have died early but he passed away with typhoid. Those days there was no cure for it."

Whether genetic or an unfortunate stand-alone case, Medha's childhood had little to suggest that the murmur heard in her heart could be indicative of a life-threatening disease. "The murmur I had was benign," repeated Medha. "It was not something that dogged me or bothered me. I just did routine checkups, that's all. Because of my mother, hospitals and doctors were commonplace for me, it was not a big deal.

"I was sensitive and events like my father's death did affect me, I still get affected by such happenings around me. But I am basically a happy-go-lucky person. I was never a brooder, not the sort to sulk or go into a depression."

The basic tendency to not let setbacks cloud the happiness of the moment was one of the many childhood qualities that remained with Medha. Easy laughter, a sunny disposition and a thirst for draining every ounce of happiness that life had to offer, marked Medha's personality as a child – and these remained her prominent traits in later years too, when she confronted the stark truth of her condition.

There were other qualities also that showed up early in life and indicated how she could cope with a roller-coaster ride that would have destroyed the morale of most other chronically-ill patients.

One such feature was Medha's determination to go for whatever she wanted, even if it meant going against her family. Looking at her delicately framed face, you wouldn't have thought that what lurked underneath was a fiercely independent personality.

It surfaced when she chose a childhood friend with a background that was vastly different from her own. Childhood friend Tani pulled no punches when she discussed the yawning gap between their families. "I came from a very outspoken communist family while Medha came from a very old, established family who had made their wealth by maintaining business relations with the British.

"What bonded us was a sense of loyalty and justice, and a rebellious streak. She was very polite, very pretty but she would give the teachers the same trouble as I did. If a new teacher asked us our names, in all seriousness I would say, 'Mayavati' and she would say, 'Kalavati', or something crazy like that. There would be bedlam in the class! Or, we stole bikes from the boys' cycle shed. It wasn't like we were smoking or drinking but just having a whale of a time and being quite boisterous. A lot of teachers loved that. In fact, to many of them, the whole batch was known as the 'Tani-Medhawala' class. A lot of them have kept in touch with us, even the nursery teachers, while they have little contact with our other batchmates. We have also reciprocated their sentiments. For instance, when a teacher dies, we go to the family, arrange a memorial meeting and so on. When the school doesn't do it, we take it on, badger them to let us use the premises and do it more aesthetically.

"But there was very deep, mutual distrust between the two families. My family would say, these *comprador bourgeoisies aise hi hotey hai*; they are all the same, while her family would feel that everything they feared about communists was coming true."

But the two friends continued to stand together through thick and thin.

If Medha chose a confidante that her family wasn't entirely comfortable with, she also showed early in life that she was not going to fit into any pre-set mould.

Tani picked an incident from the past as a sample. "The prefects were going to be announced in school. Medha was the obvious choice but there was another girl, the boring kind, who would suck up to the teachers. Both of them were made prefects but ultimately Medha didn't accept the post. She agonised over it for a week, even fainted in school, and finally, without explanation, withdrew from it, saying, '*Yeh sab bakwas hai;* it is a load of rubbish.' To this day, she has never told me why she withdrew from it."

Medha had a simple reason for pulling out of the coveted post. "I was having too much fun and I felt that as a prefect I would have to turn all serious and responsible." She wasn't ready for it.

Mother Vimla remembered another trait that remained with Medha all her life. Her unwavering desire for standing up for what she thought was right.

"Medha was once punished in school," recalled her mother. "She was given a yellow card but she kept saying, I can't get this card." A white card was what most girls got as a mild punishment while it was the boys who normally attracted a yellow card which was for more severe cases. "Medha was given a yellow card for being rude to the art teacher but she wouldn't rest until the principal had it withdrawn. She put her foot down and had her way because she felt she was not in the wrong."

There was another incident in her growing years which illustrated Medha's natural ability to face grim reality. She had a stubborn streak, laced with the required guts to accept the consequences and the strength to own up responsibility.

It had to do with Bogo, a male Spitz, and Eeda told this story. "Only six-eight months old, he was very good-looking, sprightly, and an aggressive brat. Bogo was pretty much Medha's dog but he had a very bad relationship with MJ, my dad's mother. (MJ was short for Mataji, and all the girls always referred to their grandmother as MJ.) He used to bite her because he was very possessive of his things and his territory. There were two ways of reaching the kitchen from MJ's room but she would always take the route via our room where there were two *moda*s (cane stools) which were Bogo's playthings. He felt that area was his and when she would walk into that area, he would grab her. The modas would be lying upside down because Bogo would roll them and play with them and MJ would always straighten them. Once, he snapped at her so badly, she fell and broke her leg.

"After that, he was put to sleep. It happened one day before my parents' silver wedding anniversary. I was very young then but I remember there was a big party going on here and Medha was crying. So I also sat down and cried with her because I thought it was the right thing to do."

Kushla brought out Medha's nature when she explained, "MJ had said that day, either Bogo stays here or I. We couldn't obviously tell her to go and have Bogo stay. So Papa said, we'll give him away but Medha said, 'He's my dog, I won't give him away to someone.' She took him to the doctor and put him to sleep."

The germs of a feminist were always present in Medha and they were manifest in the rocky relationship she shared with her grandmother – it was sourced to the elderly lady's old-fashioned obsession with the male child. Medha was too spunky to stomach the discrimination.

Medha said of her grandmother, "MJ was the bane of my life. I think she used to hate us because we were all girls and my father, an only son, had only daughters. If the four of us wanted to go out for *chaat* (Indian street food) and we asked MJ for five rupees, she would never give it to us. But if my cousin Atul was there, she would give not five but ten rupees."

Yet, to this day, Medha has sentimentally held on to a one-rupee note that MJ gave her even if she shrugged it off with the comment, "I don't remember what she gave it to me for. But because she never used to give me anything, it was precious and I kept it in my diary."

That strong sense of holding on to family was one of the reasons, Medha later cited, for wanting to live on, however grave the circumstances. But, like living with death, it was a paradox; Medha, time and again, struck a path that was different from the family she was so attached to.

One would have thought, for instance, that with a working mother like Vimla and a father who wanted all his girls to go out and make their names in the world, Medha and her sisters would have made great career women. But not one of them took after Vimla.

Eeda admired her mother for it. "Mummy was involved with an organisation called the Quota Club where working women would get together and collect money for various charitable causes. She was the only one who actually did the hands-on work. Even as recently as 2008, she collected funds for Bihar Flood Relief. Mummy was fairly active until Medha had her transplant. She even came with me to New York but she slipped in the apartment, had a bad fall and hurt her leg. After that, mummy got a little shaky on her feet. Until then she was pretty active, she would take a cab from the hotel and go to the hospital. She would even argue with the cab driver that he was taking the wrong route, because she knew it so well by then." Vimla would have her saree flying prettily in the New York breeze, prompting the doctors to ask her, 'How many of these do you have?' because she wore an attractive new one every day.

Eeda went on, "After that fall in the apartment, Mummy had to have stitches on her leg and she hurt her head too. Then she had a knee surgery as well. After all this, she kind of slowed down in her activities.

"Right until her trip to New York, my mother was the only one out of us who achieved anything in life. Unfortunately, her inspiration didn't work on us. All four of us are pretty useless," she smiled.

Kirti, the quietest of the four, made the point, "My father used to be after mummy that the girls should do something in their lives." However, 'Mummy' had a typical reaction to that as she commented loyally, "They have all been so active in their marriages."

A clear 'to-each-her-own' stance in Medha's family shone through. There was less evidence of being judgemental and more of gracious acceptance, which perhaps gave Medha the courage to live life the way she wanted, even if the path she often chose was far from traditional.

"I wanted them to do whatever they wanted to pursue," nodded Vimla. "I gave Medha dance and music lessons which she picked up very well. She was also highly intelligent, especially after Class IX. Till she had to do Maths and Science, she was useless in studies. Once she dropped Maths, she started coming first."

Yet, the family didn't picture Medha as someone who would grow up and make a career for herself in a creative field.

Kushla analysed, "She was doing too many things. I was doing Bharat Natyam, she was also dancing. She was learning singing as well. At the age of 13 or 14, she was doing various things, not focussing on any one activity. When she joined college at 16, she decided to do an ordinary BA pass course which was very disappointing. I said, 'Do BA Honours in Economics, or English or anything, you have the intelligence.' But it didn't seem like she wanted to go into any career. Those days not everybody was career-oriented."

Kushla did architecture; Kirti did a dietician's course. "We tried to make Medha also specialise in something but she wasn't interested," commented her mother.

Kushla remembered that even when Medha was keen to pursue singing seriously, she didn't want to do it professionally. A graceful dancer, Medha had formal training in Bharat Natyam and performed in dance dramas like Ramayan and Mahabharat that were organised by Mr Narendra Sharma in their school.

"She was very comfortable on stage but she wasn't ambitious. She learnt German, she went to FTII in Pune and did a film appreciation course. She wanted to learn many things but never concentrated on doing just one thing," concluded Kushla.

Medha agreed that she actually loved the stage and once she came to Mumbai, she did do *Bahuroopani*, an IPTA play written by Kaifi Azmi. But she didn't give theatre either the priority it needed.

Medha confirmed, "I had no great ambitions. There was no driving ambition to achieve anything. I was a pretty mediocre child until I dropped Maths and then started coming into my own. I used to learn Bharat Natyam but after the heart murmur, I was asked to go easy with it and not push it. My father introduced me to classical music.

"I was only 18 years old when he died. My father had wanted to send me abroad to study but I was never interested too deeply in any one subject to spend so much money, go out of the country and study it. I loved literature in college; I enjoyed Shakespeare, poetry, Hindi. I graduated from Lady Shriram College, did an accounts and secretarial course, and got my first job."

Meanwhile, the first big romance also happened. Medha not only fell in love but had a grand engagement as well. She dispassionately traced the romance right up to its amicable breakup.

"I had my first brush with romance in college. It was my first love experience and I took it very seriously. Vicky Mohan and I went around for five years and even got officially engaged. But, at the last minute, I decided I wanted to do more things in life than just get married."

The breakup, without melodrama, of her first romance was more or less the same way Medha handled most of her relationships. A willingness to call it quits without regret or rancour and to squarely face the consequences. In fact, most times she ended up being friends forever with an estranged partner.

"The breakup of the engagement was not at all traumatic," Medha reiterated. "Vicky and I were in the same school and college.

Doctor goes to Denmark – Medha (on dad Vijaya Gujral's right) and siblings before Vimla went abroad

Centrestage, as always – playing Draupadi in school

Close bond with music – Medha goes classical in 1971

The graduate – Medha, 1976

Childhood chapter – with best buddy, Tani

Short-lived engagement – to Vicky in Delhi

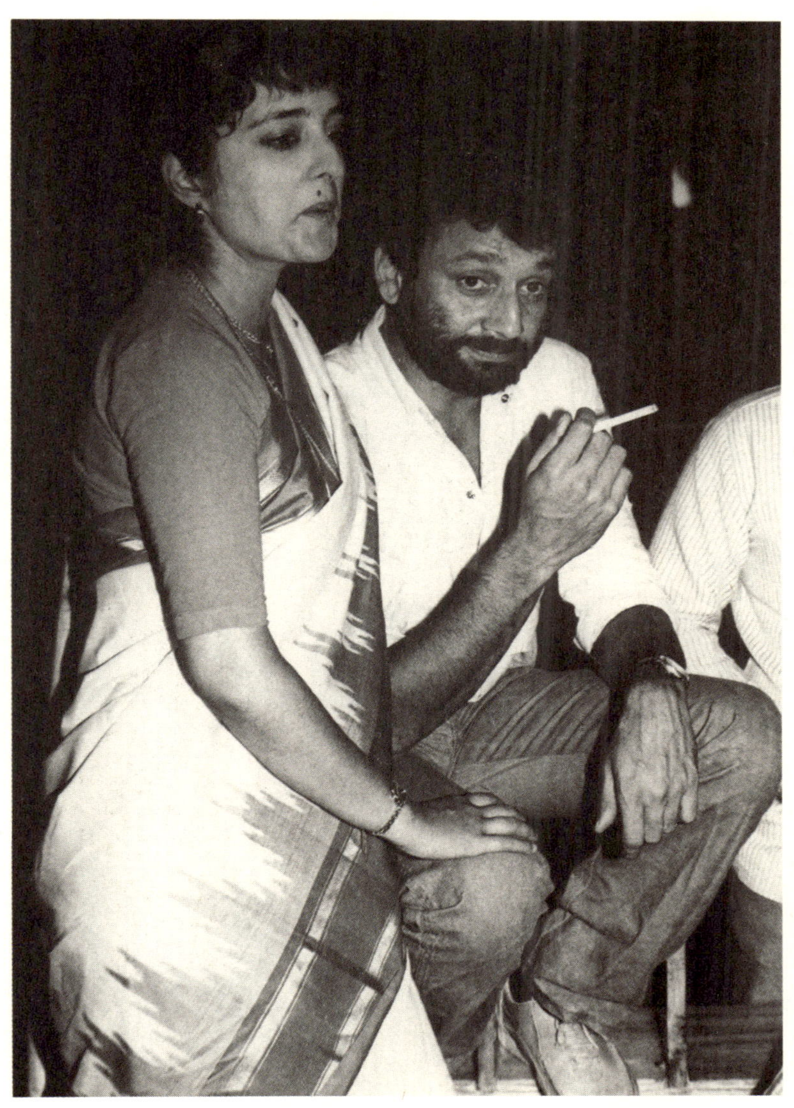

Marriage that went up in smoke – Medha and Shekhar Kapur

'Holi' hues – before Anup and Medha went official

Pre-nuptial underwater – in Mauritius

God, we've done it – temple wedding in London

NEW YOR

Unconventionally bubbly – champagne lunch at Pizza Hut after the wedding

Surprise, I'm pregnant – holidaying in Holland in 1995

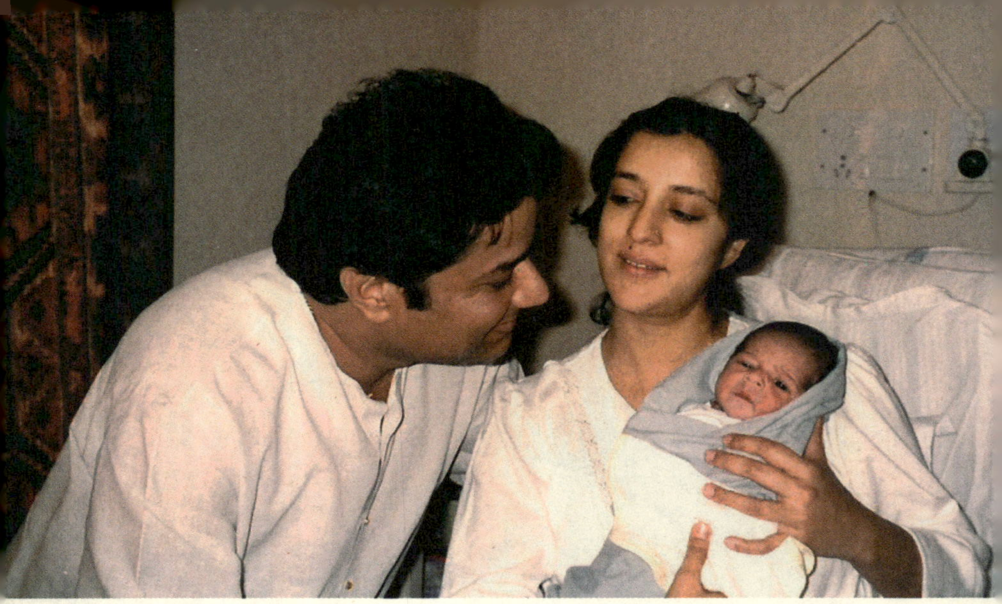

The first miracle – Aryaman arrives

Bless hubby with bliss – Medha's first Karva Chauth

Romeo on the road – Anup goes dramatic

Health and happiness – Medha and Anup on their 5th wedding anniversary with Pandit Jasraj, Kaifi and Shaukat Azmi

Calm before the storm – in California, October 1999

The romance happened in the 2nd year of college and it should have ended there but we got serious about it.

"We're still in touch," she went on. "He is married to a second cousin of mine. He surprised me a few years ago by turning up on my 50th birthday. Vicky was a very nice guy but he wasn't the right guy for me to get married to. I was 18 when I met him, 22 when we got engaged and we broke up by the time I was 23. My father was alive when it began. I was very close to my father, so he was the first person to whom I spoke about Vicky."

Medha's mother also talked of the broken engagement with remarkable calm. "Suddenly she matured more than him. But they are still good friends.

"We felt a little bad when they broke up but it was her choice. I was never bothered about what people would say. I'm not very traditional in my thinking. It depends on the girls and what each one wants out of life."

Surprisingly, the only one who was affected by the breakup was Medha's youngest sibling, Eeda, who candidly admitted, "When Medha broke up with Shekhar much later in life, I was too busy getting married to react much to it. I was more devastated when she broke up with Vicky. I really liked him and used to tie a *rakhi* (sacred thread tied on a brother's wrist by a sister) on him. I had quite a good relationship with him. Even today, I'm in touch with him. I recently spent a holiday with him and a few other people."

Kushla also stated, "All of us still meet Vicky socially."

Without chest-beating announcements, Medha sailed a choppy, colourful sea of relationships right until she anchored with Anup Jalota.

Like the Bennett siblings, Medha's sisters may have led vastly different lives but they closed ranks and shared one another's experiences.

Eeda amusedly narrated an incident that happened rather early in Medha's life. "Vicky and she must have gone somewhere and they came back very late at night, it must have been about 3 or 4 in the morning. We were all awake and he was still around when MJ woke up to check out what was happening. Vicky was quickly shoved into the loo! So Medha has had quite a few adventures."

"Medha had a tumultuous relationship with boys," buddy Tani said tartly.

The chiselled, classic Indian features and the animated glow on her face made Medha an irresistibly attractive girl, her good looks registering on everybody except herself. "I was never conscious of my looks," Medha remarked. "Girls at Modern School did whatever the boys were doing. We didn't even have enough mirrors at home to keep preening or to discuss clothes and make-up.

"Now I have become a little conscious of my fading looks. My age doesn't bother me, I love ageing and I have never hidden my age. But I have become rather conscious of my ill health, conscious that I should not look sick, gaunt or too thin."

In the unconventional Gujral family, it was not Medha's broken engagement or any other relationship that created ripples. The first upheaval in this essentially Delhi-based family came with Medha's decision to go to Mumbai on her own.

"I was already married by then but my mother was sceptical about Medha's move," said Kushla. "She worked with Thai Airways first and then with Sita Travels. I'm not sure why she wanted to go to Mumbai. We were a little scared but my mummy's younger sister was there, so we felt at least there would be someone around if she needed anything."

Her mother endorsed, "It's true that we didn't like the idea at the beginning but I never used to say 'no' to any of my daughters. Medha did what she wanted. I let all of them do what they desired. Their father was also like that. If he was so supportive of me, you can imagine how he was with the children."

As with everything else about Medha, once she had made up her mind, she got her way. She just wanted to go adventure-seeking on her own and spread her wings, perhaps unlike her father who couldn't get away. She quoted Hans Christian Andersen, "'Just living is not enough,' said the butterfly. 'One must have sunshine, freedom and a little flower.'"

Medha had no doubts dogging her about her move to a new city. "I wanted to do things on my own, stay as a paying guest, work. And I didn't want to be 'shown' any boys because my folks had begun doing that in Delhi."

The shift didn't intimidate Medha, it excited her. "I have always been a positive person, basically a happy one. I love people and I love travelling within India. I did a lot of adventurous things like going to the Pushkar *mela* (fair)."

It was this love that made Medha the first Gujral girl to break away and seek a life of her own in Mumbai. "There was a bit of a skirmish when I shifted to Mumbai and joined Sita Travels. Kirti's husband, Ashok Parashar who was with Air India, did his bit to try and sabotage my move." But once he saw how determined she was, it was Ashok who helped her find a job in Mumbai.

Kushla explained, "Ashok didn't have sisters, so he tended to be a bit over-protective of all of us."

Medha, on the other hand, was the rebel who couldn't be quelled. "I remember Ashok and Medha had the biggest fight ever," Eeda did a flashback. "I think it was just after the split with Vicky and Medha was probably in one of her rebellious phases. Ashok and Medha didn't talk to each other for a very long time."

Whatever the misgivings, once she made up her mind to go to Mumbai and step out of the fold, she not only went independent in every possible way, she also became the Page 3 celebrity in the family.

The attention she drew was not entirely due to the arrival of the suave chartered accountant-turned-actor-turned filmmaker, Shekhar Kapur, in her life. Medha always had a natural flair for basking in the spotlight. "I have hundreds of wonderful memories, especially of my childhood. I have really enjoyed every aspect of my life till this illness hounded me. I have loved life," Medha happily reminisced. She made friends, a wide variety of them. Life was full of exclamations!

"I worked for three to four years, then took a break and went to study German in Pune. There I had these roommates with whom I'm still in touch. It's a 30-year friendship and we don't have similar backgrounds at all. One of them works with Jet Airways, a typical Mumbai girl; she's not married because she's taking care of her parents. There's another, a Gujarati, who is also a spinster in Ahmedabad and she's teaching yoga, reiki, French and German. We all came together in Pune and we still try to meet every few months and spend a weekend together."

Kushla elaborated, "I clearly remember Medha as a very popular person, even in school. There were always people around her. When she was a little three-year-old, I once walked into her art class to see what she was doing, and there were these five boys sitting around her. That was so cute. She has always been very popular, very happy and perky, always doing something." Tani noticed, "A certain flightiness in Medha. I would say it set in after the breakup with Vicky and before going to Mumbai. She took some time to find her feet, to figure out whether she should buy into this story of being glamorous." She added, "Medha was born glamorous; she must have been glamorous even in her nappies!

"In the travel trade you have to be presentable," Tani pointed out. "Quite consciously, Medha kept the westernised style of dressing open for herself, something none of her sisters followed. Much after Medha, Eeda started getting westernised a little bit. Kushla and Kirti never did, even though Kirti lived for many years in Hong Kong. Medha cut her hair, wore bangs and bell bottoms, things you wouldn't associate with her now."

Medha always had such an aura around her that Eeda remembered being in awe of her. "Medha was rebellious, the black sheep," reported Eeda. "I was not as big a black sheep as she was. Considering all of us had the same upbringing, she was the only one who had the courage to leave home and build a life of her own away from the family. She always showed her courage in different ways."

But Eeda did not necessarily grow up worshipping Medha. There was a lot of resentment too, about the diva-like sibling, and Eeda was honest enough to admit, "Right through my school, right through my home life, I was always, always compared with her because I was born just after her. I was an absolute antithesis of her. She was good in studies, I wasn't. She was good in theatre and ballet and all that. I was all right at it but I hated the constant comparisons with her. I swore to myself that I would never ever compare my daughter to anybody.

"Now I have recovered from that complex and I don't really care. But strangely enough, while on the one hand I resented the comparison, on the other hand, I secretly wanted to do what Medha did. I completely admired her for going to Mumbai and staying on her own when she was about 24. I was in my teens when she left Delhi.

"I used to look up to her as a role model and admired her for doing and achieving what she did. I did higher Hindi in school because she had done it. And I got stuck with it because I had to take it up in college also. Like Medha, I also did only an ordinary BA. She did a film appreciation course in Pune and I followed suit."

Early signs of having the spotlight trained on her got amplified when Medha became a full-fledged celebrity in Mumbai. The celebrity quotient trickled into all their lives in Delhi as well.

Medha soon became the talking point of the Delhi crowd. As Eeda put it, "Because Medha was part of the celebrity circle in Mumbai, people were always asking, 'Oh, is Medha in town?' They were a little enamoured, friends, relatives, everybody. Even now, they always ask about her. Of course, today it has slightly changed. Now they enquire more about her health."

What was Medha like before she became a recognised celebrity? A bully, someone used to getting her way all the time, someone who was used to attention?

"All of it," responded Eeda candidly, "and she had all these qualities even before she was married to a celebrity. Some people just have it. Maybe it's just as well that she has this attitude – the attention, the getting her way – because what might have seemed negative at one time is actually seeing her through such a tough period of her life. I also feel that the fact she's not getting away with anything now is perhaps because it was all clubbed into her earlier years. God gave her the kind of personality that could see her through all this. If I were in her situation, even with a supportive family, I would not have had the strength to go through so much."

To return to the point where Medha moved independently to Mumbai, it was a providential shift because that's where she slipped into a role that she was eminently cut out for – that of an attractive celebrity wife with pursuits and passions of her own.

6

L'affaire Shekhar Kapur

1981, Mumbai

Medha had been with Sita Travels for barely three or four months when Shekhar Kapur entered her life. "He was making *Masoom* and he wanted someone who could write Hindi, so I joined him. We would sit on the script with Gulzar *Saab,*" said Medha of her first brush with the film industry, which was also her debut foray into Mumbai's celebrity circuit.

"Shekhar was from my school in Delhi but he was 10 years older than me. His younger sister, Sohaila, was a year senior to me. I knew him as an ex-Modernite and I knew Sohaila as well. She was also into dance in school like me.

"Shekhar was in touch with a friend called Sanjeev Bhargav (Tani's brother-in-law) whose family used to distribute films. He was the one who played Cupid and told Shekhar, he should marry me.

"I got married to Shekhar on December 19, 1981. I was 26 years old. We tied the knot as soon as the shooting of *Masoom* was completed and the post-production of the film happened after our marriage.

"Shekhar and I got married in Delhi. We had a typical, *dhoom-dhaam,* big, fat Punjabi wedding which caused a traffic jam on the road. Initially, my mother had not been very happy about the age difference but she was very happy with everything else."

"Shekhar and Medha first met at our place. Shekhar was looking for his roots," recalled Tani. "My brother-in-law, Sanjeev, who looks after the family's distribution business, distributed *Masoom*.

"Naseeruddin Shah (who went to the National School of Drama in Delhi) was an old friend of the family, then Shabana became a friend and through Shabana, Shekhar came into the picture. Medha was at a loose end at that time. When she and Shekhar met at our place, the chemistry was instant. And before we knew it, they were talking marriage.

"It was a whirlwind romance and marriage. The common ground between Medha and Shekhar was that they were both Punjabis, *Dilliwale*, Arya Samaji, Modernites, with doctor parents. It all happened quickly and it worked out very nicely."

But the several common points between Medha and Shekhar didn't make it any easier for her mother and sisters to instantly welcome her decision to get married.

"We were not upset but wary because he was an actor," explained Vimla Gujral.

Kushla was more forthcoming about why they found Shekhar the unsuitable boy. "When I first heard about Medha and Shekhar, my husband, Raman, and I said, 'Shekhar? Oh, no!'" remembered Kushla with a smile.

"My husband knew him very well from their University days. Shekhar was a year senior to me in school but I didn't know him too well. He was not very outgoing then. I think he had been suppressing himself because he was the Head Master's nephew. He was a superb swimmer, and if I'm not mistaken, was the Sports Prefect, at one time.

"So initially it was, oh, no! But we came around very fast. We are quite an accepting family that way. Once Medha was sure she wanted to marry him, all of us were behind her as we wanted her to be happy. He was also so nice to everyone that we took to him easily. He was very nice with the kids too, and soon none of us had anything against him. Even after Medha and he broke off, when he would come to Delhi, he would come and chat with mummy for one or two hours. He didn't have to do that."

Medha felt that her match with Shekhar was perfect enough to have been an arranged match. "Ours was a love marriage but it could easily have been an arranged match because we were from very similar backgrounds. His father, Dr KB Kapur, was a paediatrician, so was my mother. They knew each other; they would meet at conferences and so on. Shekhar and I had studied in the same school, went to the same Gymkhana Club. We were brought up pretty much the same way. Shekhar's *Taaya*, his father's elder brother, was the principal of Modern School.

"When I met Shekhar in Mumbai, I had no particular interest in cinema. In fact, I hardly saw any films. I must have seen my first film when I was 10 or 12. I used to find cinema halls dark and dingy and would want to keep going to the rest room. So, whoever took me to the theatre used to get angry because they would have to keep taking me out of the hall. I was very unlike my son Aryaman who has been inclined towards films since the age of seven or eight. He wants to see every film and wants to see it the first weekend itself.

"But *Masoom* was a great experience. My knowledge of Hindi and the little theatre work I had done in Delhi was put to good use. I also wrote for and worked with Goldie Uncle (Shekhar's filmmaker uncle, Vijay Anand) for a while.

"I remember meeting Shekhar first as Sohaila's brother. He was looking for locations and he found a lot of them in Delhi. One was Modern School, where he and I had studied. I had just finished doing a play as an ex-Modernite while he was not in touch with the school. He freaked out seeing the corridors and went all over the place. The school is really beautiful, it was used in the film *Rang De Basanti*. The All India Radio in the climax of the film was our school building."

Medha's transformation from a Delhi girl to a Mumbai celebrity came with some extra baggage, not all of it completely pleasant.

Eeda had her own reasons for remembering Medha's entry into the celebrity world with mixed feelings. While there was elation, there was also the bewilderment of watching a vastly changed Medha.

She described what she had found disturbing. "When Medha was with Shekhar, I used to go and meet them quite often. We would go on the sets of *Mr India* and we also went to the shooting of *Joshilaay* in Ladakh. Mummy and I went to Ladakh and there we found Medha distancing us from the shoot. She would keep us a little apart from the main scene of action."

It disturbed her enough for Eeda to return to Delhi and write to her that the trip was nice but that she found Medha strangely aloof. That was when Medha wrote back to her sister explaining that it was her way of dealing with the situation because she did not want the producer to think her family was there to take advantage of his hospitality. She did not want anything to be misread or misrepresented.

Except for these little hiccups that life in the public eye tends to throw one's way, Medha's celebrity status opened the doors to a whole new world of excitement. "*Masoom* was happening in

Delhi and I was very excited," Eeda re-lived it all. "I used to have a lot of junk in my room, a Rajesh Khanna poster, a rucksack and lots of other things, which got used in the kids' room in the film. It was great fun. But going to the *Mr India* premiere in Mumbai was the most fun.

"I really enjoyed being there. I remember sitting with Shekhar's sister, Sohaila, and commenting on the other people who were there. Oh, yeah, Medha brought plenty of glamour into our lives."

"It made all us non-film types read film magazines," chimed in Kushla.

The youngest, Eeda, just lapped it all up. "I used to be very excited because I loved star-gazing and stuff. A few times I even attended some parties with Medha. Once we went for a New Year party, another time for Holi, both at Shabana's house. Then we would sit at Prithvi Theatre, catch a play and have the Irish coffee there."

Kushla also enjoyed her share of the limelight. "I had organised a charity premiere of *Masoom* in Chandigarh for a children's hospital," she remembered. "Shabana, Shekhar, Medha and Jugal Hansraj were all there. There was a lot of excitement over their presence."

The excitement ended when Medha dropped the clanger that she was splitting from Shekhar.

Tani made the pertinent point that characteristically, Medha had been unafraid to see the incompatibility very early in the marriage.

Medha had begun to see the chinks in Shekhar's armour without ever going into battle with him. On that period, Tani observed, "Medha would say things like, 'When my *guruji* (esteemed teacher) comes, he sits pointing his feet at him. He's not interested in classical music.' I said, you can't make or break a marriage for reasons like that. But once she made up her mind, she was pretty stubborn about seeing it through. Shekhar, poor fellow, was pretty bemused and had no clue what was happening, at first. The breakup didn't happen in a well-paced, thought-out manner."

The split didn't go down well with Vimla who had grown rather fond of her celebrity son-in-law. "Shekhar used to look after Medha well. I would visit them in Mumbai or they would come here. It didn't feel nice when she wanted to divorce him but they wanted to break up. I advised her to try and make a go of it."

As with all other decisions made by her daughter, Vimla didn't stand in the way after initially dispensing her motherly wisdom.

What pleased her was that Medha and Shekhar remained friends even after their breakup. "When she fell ill, he would keep enquiring about her. At that time, he had also helped her financially," Vimla added approvingly.

Kushla repeated an earlier observation, "Medha is friends even with her ex-fiancé, Vicky. We meet him a lot at Delhi parties and he's very affectionate with all of us. Medha has always been very positive in her approach to her relationships."

She was certainly very positive that she wanted to get out of her marriage to Shekhar.

Medha vocalised a thought that had guided her through life: "When I look around, I find that people are so insecure that they're unable to accept change easily. They want to remain clinging to their negative situations even though these make them unhappy. They're afraid of trying out new things which could offer a better version of life."

She was unafraid to go out and get herself a better version of life.

"When I wanted to separate from Shekhar, my mother was not happy. But she could see that I was unhappy and left it to me to take a decision," Medha said. "Mine was the first divorce in the family. But it was not ugly, so it was okay," she shrugged.

The decision to go their separate ways was reached by Medha and Shekhar the same way that they had decided to get married.

Here's how the two life-changing decisions were reached: after they had begun seeing each other, one evening, Shekhar had fetched Medha from Sita Travels in Nariman Point and they had walked for a long while right up to Chowpathy. Shekhar had told Medha, "On our way to Chowpathy, we'll discuss all the pros and on the walk back, we'll talk about the cons. At the end of the walk, let's take a decision." That was his way of proposing to her and after their walk, they decided to trot up the aisle. Similarly, before they split, when they wanted to reach a decision on the divorce, they went to Samode Palace in Rajasthan for a long weekend, the exact opposite of a honeymoon. Shekhar wanted to know why they should split when neither was interested in marrying again and he was concerned about how Medha would manage as a single woman. She felt that since they were both going nowhere in this marriage, it would be better to divorce each other. They returned after making up their minds to make it an official, legal split.

Even before the trip to Samode Palace, what had clinched it for Medha was a certain insensitive streak that she had perceived in Shekhar. It was demonstrated when Kushla lost her husband, Raman, to kidney failure on Diwali day. Medha and Shekhar had flown to Delhi and she reeled back hurt when, instead of condoling with the bereaved, he toddled off to spend Diwali with his family. "He was married to himself," realised Medha. It was in sharp contrast to Medha who had kept up appearances that they were still a couple even after they had split, because Shekhar had lost his mother, Sheela Kapur. Medha had kept up the charade of being the daughter-in-law of the house and had continued living with Shekhar for a couple of months, until the bereaved son could find his bearings again.

But, much like her broken engagement, the divorce too, left no emotional scars on her. Medha detailed the breakup in her usual forthright manner. "It was a very clean and easy separation with Shekhar. In fact, we even forgot to get divorced, just like I later forgot to get married to Anupji. Our divorce came through six months after I started living with Anupji. I met Anupji in June and in December Shekhar and I went to Delhi to file for our divorce. Shekhar wanted it filed there.

"There was a misconception that something was wrong with me which was why I couldn't have a child with Shekhar," she paused to explain. "The fact was, midway through our 9 or 10-year-old marriage, I knew that this was not working out. He was very busy and he was married to himself. I had some gynaecological tests done and I was told that my tubes were blocked. So I told the doctors to let them remain that way.

"Shekhar loved the idea of having a child," she disclosed, "but didn't push me for it. I didn't really want one while he who wanted one, wasn't around for it. He was always travelling so much. I wanted my marriage to be in order first before I could think of a kid. My mother did ask me why I didn't have a baby and I told her, 'Let my marriage steady itself.' When Shekhar and I decided to part, it was I who wanted to break it. So I moved out.

"For the divorce, Shekhar and I went to Tis Hazari. Once there, we got interested in the lovely old architecture of the building. We were amicably sitting and having coffee, prompting people around to ask us if we were sure we wanted to get divorced. The fact was, we were still friends and had drifted apart only because there was nothing exciting me about the relationship anymore."

One of Medha's philosophies has been, "Life's too short to live it dishonestly."

Facing life's rocky stretches head-on was a speciality that had guided Medha through the various twists and turns of life. When her tubes were blocked, preventing an easy pregnancy, there was no question of keeping it from Shekhar. For that matter, even her heart murmur was discussed with Shekhar – and his folks – before their marriage.

"Of course Shekhar knew about the blocked tubes, he knew about the murmur too," remarked Medha for whom the thought of deception or secrecy had not even crossed her mind. "His father, a doctor, had even checked me out before marriage and told Shekhar that I may not be able to have a child. I talked this over later with Anupji and his family too.

"I was officially divorced from Shekhar in December 1994. Until then, we hadn't bothered to divorce each other, though Shekhar was seeing Suchitra Krishnamurthy those days. But in 1994, I wanted to get married to Anupji and after our official divorce, he too married Suchitra."

That the divorce was completely by mutual consent (they even shared the same lawyer) is further borne out by the fact that when Shekhar was getting married to Suchitra, "He suddenly realised that he didn't have the divorce papers and frantically asked me for them, saying, 'Otherwise the Arya Samaj is not giving me the marriage certificate.' So I sent him the papers. Later, when he wanted a divorce from Suchitra, he once again didn't have the papers and asked me for a copy."

After she separated from Shekhar and before she met Anup, Medha went through an erratic relationship with Pandit Jasraj's nephew Vinod Pandit, who later married Deepti Naval but died early.

Tani had strong reservations about Vinod after she went to Mumbai and met him at her best friend's behest. According to Tani, the day Medha woke up to reality, she became almost "suicidal".

Medha realised her folly when she got a phone call from a filmmaker who told her bluntly, "I want you to know that Vinod is with Deepti Naval. The whole town knows about it but you."

True to her nature, Medha confronted Vinod without ceremony. When the relationship was called off, Tani consoled her. It wasn't the breakup that drained Medha but the betrayal that was unacceptable to the principled young woman.

The point is that both Anup and Medha had had their share of stormy upheavals before they met; when they did come together it was the perfect relationship both had been sailing towards, all their lives.

7

Anup, The Anchor

Mumbai, 1994

Strangely, Medha's heart didn't do a back-flip when she first met the strongest emotional pillar of her life, Anup Jalota. Paradoxically, let alone Medha, Anup was the one man almost all her friends and family stood united against, when she initially moved towards him. Anup, with his history of failed marriages and Medha with her own share of heartaches, seemed to be inviting yet another marital disaster. Tani served her typical candour by announcing, "Anup came so quickly into the picture that I had my reservations. I am not religious at all. So Bhajan Samrat was hardly my scene. I'm more a Kumar Gandharv and Bhimsen Joshi kind of person."

So was Medha.

Tani nodded, "Medha sings beautifully, she has very good *pakad* (grasp). In school, if she heard a tune just once, she could repeat it on the harmonium in a trice. She had a very fine ear and a good voice apart from being well-trained in vocal classical.

"When she got together with Anup with serious intention, I thought it was all retrograde nonsense – he had got married so many times – and all the stories about him couldn't be wrong."

It didn't, however, take long for Anup's earthy straightforwardness to win them all over.

"Every time he had a concert in Delhi I would tell Medha that I wanted to go and hear him," Tani recalled. "What I liked about Anup, more than his singing, was his affection for his audience and his accompanists. Someone of his stature didn't have to indulge his accompanists; most people are crude with them.

"I also liked the way Anup looked me straight in the eye, her other fellows didn't do that.

"When Rajeev, my husband, was teaching at Harvard, Anup stayed with us and took us to his concert. I was always waiting for the worst to happen between Anup and Medha. I would always feel anytime he will break, anytime he will show his true colours but fortunately he proved me wrong each time.

"Today, I appreciate his complete matter-of-fact equanimity. Every time I ask about Medha, he says, '*Bilkul theek ho jayegi* (she will be perfectly all right).' This kind of positivity can lift anyone's heart. It must be uplifting for her as well."

Medha's mother and sisters also had their initial apprehensions about her new man, mainly because he had been married twice before.

Displaying her usual pliant nature, Vimla Gujral accepted the relationship and subsequent marriage even if there was nothing conventional or traditional about it. She accepted with grace, "They didn't have any ceremony here. So I did a *havan* (sacred ritual) at home for the two of them."

In any case, the Gujrals were never inclined to be a *pucca* (rigid), traditional Punjabi family.

"No, we're not," Kushla shook her head. "All of us have had love marriages."

The initial resistance to Anup was soon relegated to the past. If Vimla later held anything against her son-in-law who did a reversal of the *Savitri-Satyavan* roles and brought his spouse back from the gods of death, it was that he kept travelling and wasn't always by his ailing wife's bedside.

On the other hand, Kushla understood that he travelled because, "That was his job."

Vimla drew comfort from the fact that Medha and Anup were very happy together and, "He never holds a grudge against her."

More than anything else, all of them put a premium on Anup's calm strength and intense positivity. Kushla thought aloud, "He's very *shaant* (quiet, calm), very positive. Even if he is terrified and shaken, which he was during the first surgery when she had to get her valve changed, he would still talk very gently, very calmly. It was always very reassuring."

There was a touch of apology when Kushla accepted, "Our initial apprehensions were based on whatever one had read about him, we didn't know the real person."

Eeda, however, was the one who had no reservations about Anup right from the beginning. "He was always a really nice guy. When he moved in with Medha, it didn't shock me, it wasn't even a consideration. Maybe I was a bit amused initially but I had met my second husband by then and I was too preoccupied with my own life. Besides, I had just had my child."

Medha agreed that by the time Anup and she began living together, her mother was beyond getting shocked. She had got used to her celebrity daughter's ways. "Yeah, to her wayward ways!" Eeda laughed with sisterly cheek.

The only person who may still have been a little concerned was Ashok, Kirti's husband, who had always been rather protective of his sisters-in-law.

But by and large, Medha had it her way again and living-in with Anup was accepted without a fuss. By the time they legalised their relationship, any vestige of resentment that may have lingered had vaporised without a trace.

In fact, if Medha got a fourth lease of life, the Gujrals credited much of it to Anup's serenity.

Eeda contemplated, "To a great extent, Anup has the right kind of attitude to deal with the situation he has to constantly face at home. He has a very simplistic way of looking at things which works well for him. Whenever we ask him what the doctors are saying, his answer is, *'Sab theek ho jayega'* (everything will be perfectly all right). It is not just rhetoric, he actually believes it.

"There was one time when Medha was really critical in December, 2007. He had to go out on a concert and all of us were stunned: how could he leave her and go away at such a critical time? 'But she's going to be fine,' was Anup's only reply. I had just read *The Secret* at that point of time and I felt, maybe that's how it works, it's the power of positive thought. And I began to see the situation from his point of view."

Eeda analysed the spark of romance that has stayed alive in a marriage which has seen more hospital beds than honeymoon suites. Admiring her brother-in-law's unwavering devotion to his wife, Eeda observed, "Maybe some men would have even walked out on such a situation. I guess that must be what love is all about. I think Anup keeps his sanity by doing his programmes, by going ahead and doing what he has to. To that extent, his extensive travelling works for them.

"Sometimes I even wonder, if Medha had not been married to Anup – if she were still married to Shekhar, for instance – would any other man have been able to support her so unstintingly? I don't think Shekhar would have had the kind of time and patience that Anup has."

Eeda also traced Anup's calm dignity to his father, the late Purushottam Das Jalota, who was such a gentle person that he inspired respect.

Fortunately, Anup inherited his father's calm personality along with the musical genes which the Bhajan Samrat honed into a meditative art. His sisters-in-law unanimously believed that it was his lifelong, passionate rendering of bhajans that built up his devotion and gave him enormous reserves of strength.

While Anup had to prove his credentials to an anxious circle of family and friends before winning over the Gujrals, Medha herself was not exactly bowled over at her first encounter with him. It began with Medha's typical nose-in-the-air sneer at his kind of music.

She described her first meeting with "Anupji" with a great degree of amusement. "In the four years between Shekhar and Anupji, I was living on my own in Versova and I got into learning classical music. I used to move around with Pandit Jasraj's circle of music students and enthusiasts. Once, we were going into town when we went past this very house (Anup's house in Shivaji Park) and all of us looked up at it. It was simply in passing and I thought, 'Nice house.' That was it.

"Another time we were attending a concert in Nehru Centre where he was also singing. We went there to have some fun. Sitting in the last row, as the seats there were vacant, we actually made fun of him. We thought of ourselves as great classical music aficionados and looked down on semi-classical compositions. I was never into bhajans or *ghazal*s (Urdu verses), I went only for folk music or classical. It was Pandit Jasraj who opened our eyes to all kinds of music and taught us to appreciate all forms of it. He would praise Lata Mangeshkar also and he gave us a wider vision.

"But those were early days when we sat at Nehru Centre making fun of Anupji. We were saying to ourselves, 'After *'Aisi lagi lagan/Meera ho gayi magan'*, a line in one of his bhajans, he will hold the note till the applause starts.' That was the first time I saw him."

Later, the same group of friends went over to visit Anup. Medha recalled, "Anupji had made a very interesting hut on the terrace above, with bamboos, lanterns and fake grass. I still remember I was wearing a *lehenga* (traditional Indian skirt) and *cham-cham* (shimmery) silver jewellery.

"He was single then but that wasn't something I gave any thought to at that time. He later told me that he had noticed me in the group. But the first time Anupji saw me was when I was with Shekhar at a Filmfare party and he confessed having admired me. Many years later, Neelam Mukherjee with whom I went for walks in Versova, met Anupji and he asked her if I had gone back to Delhi. When Neelam told him my whereabouts, he took my number and called me up."

It was strange that Medha called him Anupji while her much-older first husband was simply Shekhar, sans the '*ji*' which is applied respectfully to seniors.

"Yes, I used to call Shekhar by his name though he was 10 years older than me," agreed Medha as she went on to explain, "When I met Anupji, I was with Pandit Jasraj's group. He was a senior musician, so all of us would call him Anupji. That just stuck and it felt funny to change that to Anup later on.

"I was 39 when I met Anupji, and an official marriage didn't really matter to either of us. Anupji brought me here to his Shivaji Park house and introduced me to his mother as *'Aap ki bahu'* (your daughter-in-law). I touched her feet. Then he came to drop me at Versova and didn't return to his own house. He said, 'Now that we have decided to be together, why should you live alone? As far as I'm concerned, we are husband and wife.' He stayed with me for one year in that little house in Versova.

"His parents had told him that the next time he got married, they would shift to their place in Colaba which was under construction. Anupji was very clever. He didn't let me move in here until his parents' house was ready. He probably sensed that there would be some clash with his mother. So, instead, he moved in with me."

If the Bhajan Samrat living-in with his girlfriend seemed a contradiction, Anup himself never confused his public image with his personal life. Medha called him, "An unconventional man. The image he has of this bhajan singer is at variance with what he really is. For him, it's not the norms of society that matter but what he thinks is good and correct. He's the last one to be ritualistic or to go to temples."

They met for lunch at his place on June 5, 1994. He proposed to her the same day. "Within ten days, I said 'Yes' to him. That was on June 15, 1994," documented Medha. "And we had a temple marriage in London in August, 1994."

Earlier, her mother had got them to casually formalise their relationship in her presence. "It was my birthday on June 25 and we had gone to Delhi to meet my mother. She arranged a havan, had a small ceremony, made us exchange *jaymala*s (garlands) and was satisfied that we had done something to formalise our relationship.

"To begin with, my mother had been apprehensive about his age. Anupji's image and his girth made him look older, though he was only two years older than me. The family and the many differences in our background also mattered to her. But he was a well-travelled man and the strangest of matches have worked out well in this world. It was really music that brought us together.

"After Shekhar and I separated, I had moved into my own apartment in Versova. I had begged, borrowed and stolen to buy it, and I lived there for four years. I was still working in Shekhar's office because a lot of my money was invested there. We had a little editing studio with some equipment. Shekhar had asked me to continue working with him even after we were separated." That was when the first miracle happened in her life. At the age of 40, Medha who had not conceived a child in her younger years, became a mother naturally, without any medical intervention.

"In the four years that I was living on my own, I had got into a whole lot of holistic stuff like yoga and reiki. I feel all that probably opened up my tubes by the time I met Anupji. Within a year of being with him, I was pregnant," she put on record.

If Medha and Anup lived as a couple without the formal "I do", they continued to live by their own rules, later too. Medha unabashedly revealed, "We consider August 5, 1994 as our marriage because we never really got married properly. I had done a lot of pre-marital trips with him to Mauritius and England. One day, when we were in London, the lady who organised Anupji's shows there, asked us if we wanted to get married the next day. He asked me and I said, 'Okay.' Our marriage happened as casually as that.

"The lady took us to a south Indian temple in London, she arranged for fresh *malas*, got me a red *odhni* (shawl-like scarf) from the Indian market, she brought flowers, confetti, cake, *pedas* (sweets), she even found out the right *mahurat* (auspicious time).

So we had a temple wedding. After that we had a Pizza Express lunch with champagne. Most unconventional!"

Not quite what the Barjatyas and Yashraj would call the ideal Indian wedding but Medha and Anup were content enough to discuss having a baby.

Around May-June 1995, Anup had a lot of professional commitments which required hectic travel. So he told Medha that after Diwali towards the end of the year, they could go to reputed south Mumbai gynaecologist, Dr Soonawala and check out what the problem was. But long before Diwali, much to her delight, in June 1995 itself, Medha found herself pregnant.

It was a happy coincidence that at precisely the same time, they also got themselves legally pronounced man and wife. It happened this way: after the temple wedding Anup and Medha had not bothered to get officially married. Fortunately for them, one day Anup's office needed their marriage certificate for something. The two, therefore, decided to go legal and on June 16, 1995 they were officially married.

Fascinatingly, 24 hours later, Medha discovered that she was pregnant and her instant reaction was, 'Oh, good, at least our child will be legitimate!'

"I didn't know I was already three months pregnant and I had been doing such risky things," she revealed. "We had gone up to Badrinath, we had gone trekking to some caves, we travelled in a rickety Ambassador, we went to Holland, and I was climbing up and down the old windmills where each step is two-feet high."

Several miracles were to later happen in Medha's life but without a doubt, the first was the birth of Aryaman who was a gift from the gods.

"I really think it was the yoga and reiki that opened up my tubes," she repeated. "Or, maybe because I was just so happy, I got pregnant. A journalist had written that I hadn't conceived because there was a problem with my heart but that was not the reason. In fact, those days I was very active. When I was with Shekhar who was himself very sporty, I was playing badminton, going for walks and swimming.

"There was nothing to indicate a heart condition. Because of the murmur, I would go for an echocardiogram every now and then but nothing ever came up.

"Aryaman was born in 1996."

It was a joyous occasion but Medha couldn't really enjoy her baby because three weeks after his birth, she came down with tuberculosis. Too weak to carry her baby, Medha couldn't breast-feed the infant and he had to be put on Lactogen almost immediately after he was born.

During her pregnancy, the Jalotas had hired a second driver so that Medha wouldn't have to drive herself around. Little did they know that this temporary driver suffered from TB and Medha had contracted the disease from him.

8

The Heart Breaks Down

Mumbai, 2000

In 2000, four years after the birth of Aryaman, Anup Jalota's notorious planet, the one that ruled his marital life, flared up again. The idyllic marriage of Anup, who had dared to dream of permanence in this partnership, and Medha, who had stumbled in and out of serious relationships until the tag of Mrs Anup Jalota arrived with a shelf-life that she hoped was marked forever, came under the heavy influence of Saturn.

"In 1999, all of us were in the US for a concert at David Fischer Hall where Pankaj Udhas, Anup and I were all performing," recollected Talat Aziz. "After the concert, we went for dinner to a Thai restaurant in New York where everybody was joking and having fun. At that time, Medha used to light a cigarette once in a while, so she told me, let's step out for a quick smoke. She was so bubbly, she still is. At that point of time, nobody would have even thought that a serious health issue was around the corner. We had a fantastic tour, a great concert, we enjoyed ourselves immensely and it was a complete shock when a few weeks later, I got to know that Medha was suffering from a serious heart condition."

Medha remembered the beginning of the end, almost to the day. "It was in 1999-2000 that my heart condition slowly deteriorated," she went back in time. "In May, 2000, Junior, his wife Sunita, and our families, including my mother who was in good health then, went to Mussoorie for a holiday. Suddenly, I found that I couldn't climb. I was really upset because I'm a mountain person and every holiday I would, quite literally, head for the hills.

"But this time in Mussoorie, I couldn't walk and Junior had to find paths that were straight and downhill, so that I wouldn't have to climb at all. But I was just so out of breath that I knew something was seriously wrong.

"I went to a few cardiologists on my return and all of them told me that I was in for a heart failure. A heart failure does not mean that you are going to die immediately; one can live with it for many years. But you start suffering from water retention, breathlessness and so on."

Since then, Medha has lived on the brink of her last breath for so long that she was capable of a detached, clinical narration of the terrible blows that she had to take for over a decade. It included not only immense discomfort but also dire, demoralising pronouncements even from doctors of repute.

"It began with a lot of arrhythmia (irregular heartbeats) in my heart. Certain well-known doctors bluntly told me not to do anything. One very well-known, south Mumbai doctor who visited me in Lilavati Hospital, took Rs 10,000 from us and in front of me, the patient, he just tersely said, 'Forget a transplant. Nothing is going to help her, she has very little time left.'

"My mother was very angry and wondered how a doctor could talk like that in front of the patient. Fortunately, on further probing the disease, we found that a transplant could be the way out."

It was a long and arduous procedure to be on her feet again. Going to the US, "Getting a little screwed by their systems," and eventually returning home with a new heart took up two full calendar years and left their coffers more than empty.

Through it all, Anup refused to give up and Medha fought for her life, never once entertaining the thought of death because: "One, Aryaman was only four years old. Two, I felt very bad for my mom. She had already lost one daughter when my sister, Vibha *didi* had died, and I didn't want her to go through that pain again.

"More than anything else, I wanted to live because Anupji and I had ultimately found each other. Even if I live only for a short while, I can confidently say that I found my soulmate in him. After 15 years of marriage, *kuch baasi nahin hua hai,* nothing in our relationship has dulled or become stale."

Unfortunately, for the two of them, it wasn't their marriage that was failing, it was her heart that was letting them down. "After the disease began in 2000 in Mussoorie, I could feel it coming on, slowly. I was no longer very active. I was no longer exercising, swimming or playing badminton. Once I moved to Shivaji Park, there were no gyms or clubs close by. There was nothing to do except maybe walk around the park. So I was suddenly left bereft of exercise and my stamina was not on test. But I found that if I did something even slightly strenuous like climbing steps, I would be out of breath.

"When I came back from Mussoorie and began to experience arrhythmia and water retention, I went to Dr Amit Vora, an electro-physiologist and arrhythmia specialist. A genius of a doctor, he had gauged the condition of my heart accurately and told me, 'Don't go from doctor to doctor but probe a heart transplant immediately.'"

But Medha did just that – she did a disheartening round of doctors, none of whom really helped her. One of them had actually written the name of the disease on one side of the paper but had not explained it to the patient. A whole load of tests were done. An ECG threw up an anomaly, so did an echocardiogram. Finally, there was talk of going to the US, an eventuality which the Jalotas began to probe.

The whole Gujral-Jalota clan soon picked up complicated medical terms they had never heard of a decade ago. Eeda recalled, "The first time it happened, we didn't quite understand what heart failure was. My mother told me to go to Mumbai because Medha's pulse rate was fluctuating and she needed to be immediately hospitalised. But before I could reach, Medha had gone into hospital and when they started researching and investigating her case at Lilavati, one of the senior doctors told her point-blank that there was no hope for her. Nobody knew what was happening. They found that she had erratic heartbeat, arrhythmia, and later she was diagnosed with cardiomyopathy. That's when the whole process of a heart transplant started."

With no clue whatsoever of the extraordinarily long stretch of hospital stints, surgeries and life-threatening situations that lay ahead of her, Medha was so fed up of the rigmarole of illnesses and doctors' verdicts that one morning, she actually ran away from Lilavati Hospital. Anup was at the hospital with her. When he was in the rest room and the staff had changed for a new shift, Medha togged up in civvies and caught a cab home. Once in the safety of her house, she sent an SMS to her startled husband who had to go and sign 'Discharged against medical advice' papers.

It was a stand-alone incident of playing truant as Medha soon accepted the critical nature of her illness and transformed into one of the most ideal patients any of her doctors had to deal with.

When things begin to go wrong, life has a way of falling apart on several fronts. If it was unfair that Medha and Anup could barely enjoy wedded bliss and Aryaman's arrival, it was only the starting point of a long period of bad luck. One of which was the decision to go to Mayo Clinic in the US.

Through Dr Alok Chopra, one of her Delhi doctors, Medha and Anup contacted Dr Khanderia in Mayo Clinic in the small town of Rochester in the state of Minnesota. It was decided that she would get a heart biopsy done to figure out whether or not she had a disease called 'restrictive cardiomyopathy.'

"So I went to Mayo Clinic in the US," Medha re-lived the experience. "During my biopsy, they inadvertently cut off a chordae of my mitral valve and I almost went into a coma-like state. I was haemorrhaging, the blood was flowing backwards. It happens maybe once in 10,000 cases. An immediate open-heart surgery to fix that valve was the only option thereafter."

That was no quick-fix treatment, not a permanent one for sure. Even after the biopsy, Mayo Clinic couldn't conclude whether she had the disease or not.

Medha remembered it all deadpan, inured to the hammering they encountered at every turn. It was a drain on all their resources, emotionally, physically and financially. Through it all, Anup stood resolutely confident, refusing to be demoralised by the wave of setbacks.

He was ubiquitous as he held his wife's hand, ensured that their son was safe, arranged for funds and kept singing without missing a single beat.

It was during Medha's battle for survival in the US that he flagged off a weekly TV programme on bhajans which he hosted. He would religiously fly down to Mumbai to can a few episodes and return to New York by the next available flight.

After making her undergo open-heart surgery for a valve that they had accidentally messed up and subjecting her deteriorating body to a battery of tests, Mayo's verdict remained inconclusive. She was back to square one when she returned to India in August 2000.

Aryaman was four years old then and had been left in the care of Anup's sister, Anita Raje. Medha returned to India and seemed fine, now seriously doubting if she did indeed have cardiomyopathy at all.

However, in October 2000, Dr Alok Chopra, her old cardiologist in Delhi, noticed that she didn't look too well and tested the condition of her heart by asking her to climb two flights of steps with a meter on her finger that checked how much oxygen was going into her heart.

Alarmed at the result, he made Medha call her mother. "You are going into cardiac failure. I'm taking you straightaway to Escorts," said he to Medha.

"Something was very drastically wrong," recalled Medha. "It seemed I had peri-cardiac fluid around the heart. That had to be tapped out.

"I was in and out of the ICU again. My heart was in a mess. I was sometimes well, sometimes ill, and going into heart failure. Because the heart was not pumping well, fluid would develop in the belly and make me look like I was nine months pregnant. They would have to tap the fluid out."

In April 2001, the doctors in India gave up on her and sent her back to the US. Talk of *vinaash kale vipareeta buddhi* (roughly translates as, when times are inauspicious, the brain packs up and prompts you to do something illogical). "Like fools, we went back to Mayo."

Once again, the rigmarole of tests and dire verdicts swirled around her. By now Medha's condition had sharply deteriorated. "They kept doing all kinds of tests for a month-and-a-half which really cost us a packet," said the worn-out patient. Worse was to come when, at the end of it all, a group of surgeons offered her little help or hope, and simply told her, 'We're sorry but we cannot give you an extra life.' "That was the most depressing part of this whole unpleasant experience," recalled Medha. "They told me that I would need a heart and a lung transplant but since the lung pressure was not normal, I would die on the table. And they couldn't waste a heart on me."

While she coped with heart-tugging medical decisions, Medha simultaneously made sound, practical decisions. She shared an aside at this juncture. "When I was in Mayo and they were evaluating me for a transplant, I had long hair and I just couldn't deal with it. So the first thing I did was to cut my hair and donate it to people who made wigs for cancer patients."

The long stint in Mayo was a total drain on their resources. Medha, who kept a meticulous medical record of her 11-year ordeal, left the financial statements to her husband. "All I can say is that it cost us much more than we could afford. We had to beg and borrow to meet the bills.

"I had some of my own money that had come from our house in Delhi which had given way to a tall construction. Each of us got a part of it which we leased out, getting a sizeable amount of rent from it. I also had my property in Versova and in Bangalore. So I had some money of my own though I had no career or ambitions."

All the money – hers, his and some borrowed – was poured into keeping her alive. In 2009, Medha sold her Bangalore property too, to raise funds for the kidney transplant that she hoped would happen in 2012.

There were many lessons that Medha and Anup learnt from their US sojourns.

But fate has a way of opening a door when all else seems bleak. Medha talked of a sunny breakthrough that happened unexpectedly: "In Mayo I came across an Indian doctor, Dr Sunil Khushwaha, who told me that he had worked under Dr Alan Gass at Mount Sinai Hospital, New York.

"He told me that in Mount Sinai they would have never rejected a case like mine. Dr Khushwaha wrote to Dr Gass who saw me and said that they would do another evaluation of their own and then try and take me in."

It wasn't a cakewalk as Dr Gass had to fight with his seniors to get Medha into Mount Sinai. He fought for her because he was convinced that with age on her side and the rest of her body (except her deteriorating heart) in healthy condition, they could help her.

"Finally, the doctors agreed," she recalled the relief with a smile. "There was fluid in my belly, so Dr Gass said, 'We will tap you out but come prepared to stay for about two or three months. You will have to wait till we get a heart.'"

Dr Alan Gass recalled Medha's first visit to him and explained that she was diagnosed with a rare condition called 'endomyocardial fibrosis' where the inner lining of the heart becomes hard and stiff and the pressure in the lungs is far too low to supply oxygenated blood to the rest of the body.

"Mount Sinai where I was working, was doing very innovative therapies and medication, especially to get people who had pulmonary hypertension safely to a cardiac transplant. So it was kind of fortuitous that God sent her to me because Medha found the right hospital that was doing exactly what she needed."

He was completely alert to her serious condition because, if she had not got the right treatment at the right time, "She would not have made it because her heart would have continued to fail and she would have had a pretty miserable existence," he analysed with forthright precision. "Her lungs and her heart would have got worse, eventually both would have failed. She would have suffered a lot and died."

A believer would say that it was indeed God himself who sent Medha to Mount Sinai to Dr Alan Gass at the opportune moment. But the dramatic, multiclimactic coincidences that played a part at every turn of this saga continued. Unbelievably, the date she was given to check into Mount Sinai for the transplant in 2001 was 9/11! Packed and mentally geared to move into hospital to get herself a new heart, Medha recalled, "I was staying with Anupji's cousin, Radhika, in New Jersey. We were getting ready when we suddenly got a call saying, 'Don't come into Manhattan, the Twin Towers are down.' We switched on the TV and saw the second tower going down. It was so awful, everything just shut down in Manhattan. The bridges, the tunnels were all shut down, the phones were off, and I couldn't get through to my doctor. My stomach was big and uncomfortable but we couldn't do anything about it.

"9/11 continued with me right through my heart transplant. While I was in hospital, television would all be about 9/11, Osama and visuals of people in panic."

Fortunately, by the afternoon of 9/11, Dr Gass was allowed to get through to Medha on a special phone line. He directed her to a hospital in New Jersey where the tapping could be done, and told her that after a week, once everything had settled down, she could go to Mount Sinai.

When Dr Gass had first discussed the transplant with Medha, he had gently made it clear that she could go through with it only if she had staunch family support. Anup and Kushla who were with Medha assured him that the support would be unstinted. The caring physician had pointed out that the entire process, the wait, the surgery and what followed thereafter, would be too traumatic to be faced alone. "All of it was, without exaggeration, really true," noted Medha.

Once New York began to recover from the 9/11 attack and the roads opened up, Medha could finally check into Mount Sinai. But tough times still shadowed her as 9/11 had a rippling effect everywhere.

"Arranging for the money became very difficult. After 9/11, people were being laid off. Whoever Anupji would tap for some help would either be unable to or unwilling to help because nobody knew where the US was going. The economy was collapsing, airlines were shutting down because nobody wanted to travel by air anymore. It was really a bad period for the US."

Anup met the challenge and in a few days raised the required money to pay half the amount upfront before Medha could be listed for a transplant. Meanwhile, she was put on life-saving drugs in the ICCU.

Medha went in on September 18, 2001 and got her new heart on December 8. She had gone in wearing a T-shirt and she came out in an overcoat – the seasons had changed during her long hospital stint.

She marked the change from inside. "From my window, I could see the leaves in Central Park turn from green to brown and then drop, leaving behind only a bare tree."

She faced the sighs and highs of hospital life in that period. On November 27, 2001, she had a false alarm.

Medha recounted, "The transplant coordinator came into my room and said, 'We have a heart for you, so start getting ready.' Anupji had a concert in Delhi that day and with me was a friend, Simi Bhandari, who lived in DC. We were all very flustered but when we phoned Anupji, he said that he would take the first flight and be there with me. He used to carry his passport everywhere with him.

"Anupji told the concert organisers that he had to go. I was told at 12 pm that they were going to take me in at 2 pm. My friend asked me what I'd like to do for those couple of hours. Since I had already undergone a couple of surgeries, I was aware of what it was like to lie around for days and days post-operation. So I called the nurse and requested her to shampoo my hair!

"I was in an ICCU where there was a small sink in the room and because my tubes were so long, I could walk up to the basin, wash my face, brush my teeth and even bathe from it. I did all that when around 1.30 pm, the nurse came in to say, 'I'm sorry, it was a false alarm, the doctor has rejected that heart for you.' I quickly rang up Anupji who was on his way to the airport. He turned the car and went back to the wedding where he was scheduled to sing!"

Amazingly, through all this excitement, upheavals and heartbreaks, in the entire 11-year ordeal, Anup Jalota never once faltered on stage or let his audience even get a hint of his woes. His dedication to his singing, to his meditation, was complete.

Getting a heart could create such a flutter that old pal Tani also remembered the exact date of the false alarm for her own reasons. "It was on November 27, it was my daughter's *arangetram* (the first public performance by a Bharat Natyam student) and Eeda came to me in the interval and said, 'She has got a heart.'"

Medha revealed, "A false alarm like that can be really disheartening but I also knew then that I was highest on the list in the New York area. I had already been called once, so I knew that as soon as they found a match for me, I would get a heart."

All of Medha's childhood traits, of facing reality squarely in the face, of going into something with dogged determination and no thought of failure, of looking at the bright side and not allowing her spirits to flag, came to her aid once again. It was topped with Anup's Hanuman-like store of forbearance and positivity. Neither of them looked at the problem as anything but a costly impediment which had to be overcome. Son Aryaman too, posed no obstacle.

Medha, ever practical, had not mothered a clingy child. "From the beginning, we had brought up Aryaman to be very independent. In the first year that he was born, we left him at home several times. Each time we went away on our own, we left him with relatives. So Aryaman got accustomed to his parents being away for a brief spell.

"When I was in the US, one day he just turned up there to meet me. In fact, he brought me luck. Aryaman came on December 5, 2001, and I got my heart on the 8th, three days later. So he was there when I finally had my transplant.

"When we went to the US in April, 2001, I didn't know how long I would be there and I ended up being there for almost the whole year. I went into hospital in September and came out on December 28. The doctors there asked me to stay on in New York for a year after the transplant, to adjust to the medication and to go through various biopsies. Every now and then they would do a biopsy which was the only way to find out if you were rejecting the alien organ.

"Heart transplant in India was at a very nascent stage at that time. We didn't have a proper harvesting system or a proper donor system. That's why one had to go to the US for it."

All along it was only a question of recovering and returning to normalcy. It never occurred to Medha that she was in a life-threatening situation from which the chances of coming out alive were extremely slim.

Dr Gass saw that quality in her and perhaps that played its own part in his decision to take on a seemingly impossible case which so many had turned down as hopeless.

"She was young," he explained, "very young and otherwise healthy. My job was to get the pressure in the lungs down, low enough to get her safely through for surgery. That's when I instituted a specific type of therapy that I was using back then and she responded extremely well to it. That's why the surgery was so very smooth with no complications during the operation or after."

What aided the treatment was her own mental condition which he described as, "Superb".

"I could tell by looking at her eyes that she really wanted to live," he continued. "And that's why I wanted to do everything I could to help her. Her family was a big part of it, very supportive and educated. All these qualities gave me the motivation (to help her)."

"Through all this, I was in good cheer," Medha too, emphasised. "The only *dhakka* (setback) I got was at Mayo when they told me that they could not do anything for me.

"Somehow," she mused, "though I was so close to it, I never thought of death. I always felt I would pull through and come out alive.

"While I awaited a new heart, I was put on two drugs, one of which was Dopamine which helped me because I think it makes you feel a little good. The second was a drug called Natrocor which had never been used in this hospital before. It was an absolutely new FDA-approved drug. The doctor wanted to try it out on me to see if it suited me. It suited me so well that I was put on it. The pharmaceutical company that made it was following my case and it was Natrocor pads and Natrocor stationery all over my room."

The recovery almost sounded like a picnic and Medha had more fun times on memory recall than tales of pain, discomfort or trauma.

"Those three months went off quite well. The nurses were so nice to me that it began to feel like home. Only the physical discomfort was immense. For 15 days I would have the Swan-Ganz catheter inserted on the right side and for 15 days on the left. The procedure to shift it to the other side was really unpleasant." That was the maximum she recalled of the downside, preferring to be upbeat about the young new heart that she finally romped home with.

"I was told that I had got the heart of a 20-year-old who had died in an accident, like most organ donors in the US. All I was told was that he was a big guy, more than 6 ft tall. These days they don't give you even this much information because some people object that they have been given a 40-year-old heart or they start asking for a male or a female heart, etc.

"I was given a large heart because I had poor lung function. My new heart was double the size of my original one. After the transplant they left me open for four days, there was just a net covering me. They didn't stitch me up until the heart found its cavity and settled down. I was unconscious all through, knocked out for four days. In fact, they were worried *ki ye uth hi nahin rahi hai*, she's not waking up at all. I was happily unconscious.

"When I woke up, the TV was on with Osama's letter. Everything seemed fuzzy. I thought I had gone blind but it was actually Urdu lettering with sub-titles in English."

The worst was over and it was time to pop the champagne. "Aryaman was very young then, so his studies were not affected. After the surgery, when I returned to Mumbai, I was at home and gave Aryaman a lot of time. All his teachers knew about my surgery, the school had given him leave to come to the US in December and he was there right until Jan-end. He was there for his birthday on January 26, 2002. So my going away wasn't traumatic for him. But somewhere, I think the insecurity had affected him. He has seen mamma go and not come back for so long. But you know how resilient kids are. I wasn't expecting him to come to the US, it was a surprise for me. Anupji came into the hospital room on December 5 and said, 'I have a gift for you.' And in walked Aryaman. I was sitting up watching television, with all those wires around me. Aryaman gave me a hug, plonked himself on the bed, watched TV and asked, 'Is there a computer around here?' He took all those tubes and electrodes in his stride.

"There's a photograph of him and his little cousin coming to see me after the surgery. They had to wear masks because I was 'immune-suppressed'.

"Kids adjust well to situations but sometimes I can see his insecurity. Like the time I had a kidney failure in December, 2007 and was very critical for about two days. My entire family, my mother, sisters, everybody had come down. He was grown up enough by then and he must have wondered if something drastic was happening since everybody had gathered in Mumbai."

If Medha never entertained the negative thought of a tragic end and Anup convinced himself and everybody else that this too shall pass, the same positive thinking was passed on to Aryaman. Even when Medha lay critical, Aryaman was never asked to prepare himself for the worst. When his parents themselves didn't believe for a moment that the problem was insurmountable, there was no question of letting the little one treat it as doomsday.

"We never sat him down and asked him to be prepared for the worst," explained Medha. "But we have always been very honest with him about my disease." Something that the four-year-old did during his mother's transplant showed that Aryaman had understood the enormity of the situation.

Medha narrated, "When he was in the US, Aryaman would sometimes go to his cousin's school there. On New Year's Eve, all the kids were asked to say something. He went on stage and said, 'I want to thank that person who died, so that my mom could get a heart. I haven't come here for a holiday, I am here because my mother had a heart transplant. And I'm grateful to the person who died.'

"Imagine a four-and-a-half-year-old saying that! Anupji's cousin who was there said that almost everybody had a little tear in the eye."

There was much to be grateful for as life returned to normal after the heart transplant. Medha articulated her rebirth. "When I returned after the heart transplant, I felt completely renewed. Slowly but surely, I could breathe, I could walk, I could do so much. After I came out of hospital, we moved into an apartment in New York and we were there until November, 2002."

The sheer joy of breathing freely and being alive was expressed through small little acts. "When I got out of hospital and checked into an apartment, I wouldn't shut the blinds, I used to keep all the windows open and look at the world outside," Medha savoured the remembrance. "It was so wonderful to be alive. I would be on steroids but one night I was dying to have an ice cream. The very next day after I moved in, I started cooking. I didn't want to sit around doing nothing. I wanted to settle into a routine, though I couldn't do too much. I used to walk two rounds a day in the passage, then progressed to five rounds until I started going on the treadmill."

Medha may have been at death's door; the Jalotas and the Gujrals may have scraped the bottom of the barrel to settle the enormous bills but very typically, Medha talked of the entire chapter like a holiday with a difference.

"Throughout my illness, throughout my sojourn in the US, we had a really great time," she insisted. "I have never had so much time with my husband or with each friend or relative who came and spent time with me there. If I hadn't been ill, who would have spent so much time with me? Married sisters don't have that kind of time to spend two or three weeks with each other. So that was the really nice part of the illness. In New York, we would go to the museum, see a play, do stuff together. So actually we had a great time throughout. It's a wonderful way of looking at the whole experience."

"Yes, all of us went and spent time with her," nodded Kushla. "Before me, it was Kirti, Eeda went later. Mummy had planned to stay till the surgery but she broke her foot and she didn't want to be a burden on them, so she came back. But Anup and Aryaman were with her during the transplant."

Medha's startling recovery was perhaps due to her obstinacy to prove to the doctors who had given up on her that she could not be written off so easily. Tani agreed that much of Medha's strength came from her *zid,* her stubbornness which made her fight back with a spirited *main tumhe dikha doongi* and prove that she was no pushover.

The night that Medha had an urge to have an ice cream, Tani had just arrived in New York to be with Medha. It was snowing, it was a miserable night and Tani was exhausted after a long flight. At 10 pm, when Medha insisted on an ice cream, Tani was reluctant to fetch it from a deli below but she was cajoled into going out, bleary-eyed. When she returned, Medha had already fallen asleep, so Tani put the ice cream in the fridge.

"Late at night, around 2 o'clock, Medha began shouting and I was totally rattled," Tani recounted. "On those wooden floors, I skidded into her room wondering what had happened. And she said, '*Yaar* (buddy), I want that ice cream.' I was quite cross but when I gave her the ice cream, she sat me down and explained, 'You don't understand. I may be 40 years old but I have the heart of a 20-year-old guy and that heart wants an ice cream!'"

The patient had enormous fun in different ways. On one occasion, Medha's aunt, Asha *Maasi*, who had come to visit her from Australia, wanted to buy herself a wig. Medha scoured the internet and finally sourced one from a fancy shop in Broadway. "It was great fun getting that wig for her and it was hugely entertaining for me," laughed Medha. "Sadly, Asha *Maasi* passed away recently."

Recalling the fun and frolic was a stress-buster that worked for the whole family. New York was where Medha got herself a new heart and a brand new life. But even the crisis-ridden stint in Mayo Clinic had its entertaining sidelights.

Eeda recalled T-shirts there that read: 'Reconstructed in Mayo' because Mayo was a place where they changed every part inside you – the heart, kidneys, lungs, literally everything.

"Mayo is quite an amazing little place," Eeda described it well. "Everything is so hospital-oriented there. They have a labyrinth of corridors because it gets so cold and they have blood deposit banks all over the place. If you have had a blood test, you can write all the details on the envelope and just deposit the blood at a convenient 'bank'. It will go to the correct hospital and the results will come back to you."

While they waited for the results of the battery of tests conducted on Medha, the sisters treated it like a nice little vacation. "We were staying in this really sweet little bed-and-breakfast place which had only tea and coffee," Eeda detailed the stay. "We would eat lunch out and for dinner, there was a KFC and a nice little restaurant. Every evening, I would ask Medha what she wanted, pour myself a drink in a paper cup, carry it along and walk to order dinner. Then we would both sit at home and eat together. That became a daily routine.

"One day we hired a car and went off for a drive." With a tiresome wait before them while the doctors decided what they were going to do with Medha, there was little else to do but to enjoy every moment spent together.

Kushla described the hospital experiences with similar feelings of anxiety and amusement. "I was scared during the transplant because Medha was in a very bad state. But she herself was so infectiously positive that frankly, we enjoyed ourselves. Like at Mayo Clinic, when I had to push her wheelchair and my saree came in the way, she asked me why I hadn't brought a *salwar-kameez* (Indian costume with a tunic and loose pants) which was more convenient to wear. I usually wear sarees but I had packed two sets of salwar-kameez in case I needed to dress in a hurry. So the next day, I wore a salwar-kameez and as luck would have it, the *dupatta* (long, scarf-like part of the ensemble) got caught in the wheelchair."

Kushla promptly deposited her dupatta and her bag in Medha's lap and made her carry them around. It was typical sisterly fun and they enjoyed each other's company.

"Even when we had to go for her tapping, Medha would ask me to sit with her," continued Kushla. "In the US, they allow you into the ICU; in fact, they are happy if someone is with the patient and let you sit there from 8 am to 8 pm."

Kushla felt reassured as long as she stayed by Medha's side. It was when they were all far away in Delhi that fear would set in.

"When the heart-transplant surgery was going on, we would talk to Anup from Delhi every half hour," said Kushla. "Whenever a nurse or someone would come out of the operation theatre to report on the progress, he would call and update us. That was a scary time."

On December 14, sister Kirti's daughter got married in Delhi. So there were celebrations in Delhi almost simultaneously with the transplant happening in New York. The undercurrents of tension were unavoidable. Medha herself had foreseen it and had made Kirti promise that the wedding would go on uninterrupted even if something extreme were to happen to her in New York. Were there heart-stopping moments for the family during the really critical phases of Medha's treatment? Was Vimla afraid that she could lose another daughter?

"Vibha's death was different. But yes, during Medha's transplant I feared that anything could happen," Dr Gujral conceded. "I had gone to meet her in Mayo when she was very critical. They said she won't live. They refused to even do a transplant. Then she went to New York and there they agreed to do a transplant. Those were very anxious moments for us. But for five years after the transplant, everything was fine."

The family coped with the tension by simply being extremely supportive. All of them took turns to fly to the US during the various stages of Medha's long and trying treatment.

Eeda felt that Medha was fortunate because, "Right from the stint in Mayo till she had her heart transplant and returned to India, she was never alone. Close friends and family took turns going and spending a lot of quality time with her."

Anup sailed in two boats but didn't let either sink or shake. While Medha's recovery was uppermost in his mind, the focus on his career never shifted.

"Anupji kept working through all this," pointed out Medha. "We had arranged for somebody to be with me all the time. His cousin Radhika in New Jersey was a strong pillar of support. I couldn't have gone through it all without her."

In Mumbai, it was Anup's sister Anita, "Who was like an angel. She came to our house and stayed with Aryaman, so he didn't have to be uprooted. She took care of him like a mother."

The loyal domestic staff too, pitched in with unstinted support, especially Man Friday Ramchandra and cook Triloki who were with the family for years. "Having Ramchandra around was like having a father at home. I couldn't have left Aryaman behind so many times without Ramchandra's help and presence in the house."

Interestingly, Ramchandra had come into Anup's house much before Medha herself. "Actually he came in with Sonali (Anup's first wife), as part of her 'dowry'," Medha revealed with a chuckle.

However, Medha did not share a warm relationship with some of her in-laws. "For my mother-in-law, I was Anupji's third wife, so I don't really blame her," she accepted.

Medha also found Anup's younger sister in Jabalpur a little aloof and reserved. What hurt was that none of them ever called her up and enquired about her health even in the most critical of moments.

"I'm sure they were all concerned," she conceded, "and they would all talk to Anupji. But none of them ever called up and asked me how I was. That hurt me a lot."

But Medha progressed well and was able to return to India in November 2002, even if the healing process wasn't all hunky-dory.

"I had a couple of big rejections of the new heart," reported Medha. "It is quite funny because you don't even know that your body is rejecting the new organ, there are no symptoms as such. It's only the biopsy that tells you about it."

In March, Anup's younger brother and his wife were with Medha in New York when she went to the gym downstairs. "When I came up, there was a message on the answering machine saying, 'Come to the hospital immediately, you're rejecting.' Imagine, I had just been on the treadmill for half-an-hour with a heart that was being rejected!"

She was back to the hospital for three days where she was pumped with steroids and then sent home. "That was a big rejection," she kept track. "There was one more and a few small ones in between. I had chronic rejection all through."

Ideally, the doctors would have wanted her to stay in New York for one full year after the transplant. "But by November I was fed up and wanted to come back home," Medha recalled.

The doctors allowed her to fly back to India but for one year, she had to go back every month for a biopsy. Later it was once every three months, then six months and the frequency was gradually reduced.

"I left Aryaman behind so many times. But it was getting very expensive to stay on indefinitely in New York."

The biopsy itself was a tedious procedure that she had to undergo each time she went back to hospital.

"It is done under local anaesthesia," explained Medha. "They take a tiny piece of the heart through an invasive procedure via the jugular vein or groin, and check it. After the transplant it was done every week, to see if the body was rejecting the new organ.

"The procedure is for only about half-an-hour but the whole day goes on prepping, and you have to keep standing in the Cath

Lab which is like an operation theatre. After that you are a little unsteady, so you are supposed to rest. Now I'm down to one biopsy a year in which they do an angiogram too, to see if there are any anomalies."

Life was back on track by the time 2003 dawned. Medha was back to hosting parties. When Anup turned 50 on July 29, 2003, the singer and his wife had a lavish celebration at Taj Land's End where all their gifted friends like Hariharan and Talat Aziz turned it into an impromptu concert of great singing talents. The tradition continues to this day.

9

The Kidneys Fail

Mumbai/New York 2007

The picnic lasted until 2007 when the hearty health bulletins were abruptly replaced by alarming lab reports. This time her kidneys threatened to pack up. It was back to Mount Sinai in New York.

"In November, 2007, they discovered that one of my main arteries was 90 per cent blocked," Medha talked of the next phase of critical, on-the-brink moments. "That happened only because of the medication, not my diet. I have never had a bad diet. I have always been very careful about oil and fats and have never indulged in excesses when it comes to food. At Mount Sinai they had to do an angioplasty and put a stent in."

It was a disheartening experience for Medha as Dr Gass, who had guided her during the heart transplant, was no longer with Mount Sinai and a new bunch of doctors began to attend on her.

"I could feel the treatment not going well," she reminisced. "For the new doctors, I was just another patient. My kidney failure was more rapid and violent as a result, leading to a near-death situation."

Perhaps, the picture of hope that Mount Sinai represented had been disturbed by the fact that Dr Alan Gass was no longer in the frame.

"It's an interesting thought," agreed Dr Gass. "The mind is definitely connected to the heart. That's why through the ages there have been phrases like, 'My heart is bleeding' or 'My heart is broken'.

"I could see that Medha had faith in God, in a higher being. I represented a tangible intermediary between her and God; it is easier for a patient to have blind faith in someone they can hold on to, touch and feel. When she couldn't see me at Mount Sinai, maybe it had an impact on her not doing well."

The alarming state of her kidneys was a problem that Medha had anticipated. Aware that the heavy medication necessitated by the heart would eventually take its toll on her kidneys, she watched with alarm the rise in the creatinine levels in her blood reports. A moderate increase in the levels was expected but as it went higher, it spelt big trouble. In 2006 itself, she had been categorically warned by her doctors in New York that she would have to keep a watch and take care of her kidneys.

Medha did just that but hit a roadblock in the form of an insensitive kidney specialist. "In early 2007, I had started seeing a very senior specialist at Lilavati Hospital," Medha stated and charged, "He was very careless and let my kidneys deteriorate. He would call me, make me wait for an hour outside his room and then ask me to do some tests and see him after two months. He did it to me five times until I told my GP, Dr Farhad Kapadia, that I needed to change my kidney specialist. I didn't care if he was a senior, I was just not getting good vibes from the doctor I was seeing.

"When I finally went to Dr Jatin Kothari at Hinduja Hospital, he was appalled to see the creatinine levels and asked me why something had not been done about it. It was just bad luck that I had wasted so many months in the wrong hands.

"I faced a lot of problems after the angioplasty too. Another one of those things that would happen to one in 8,000 people happened to me. When the stent was put in, something went wrong. My entire right leg turned black and blue and was swollen. So they had to do another procedure to set that right. When I came back from New York, I was laid up in bed during which time the kidney problem started galloping."

Six years after she got a new life, Medha's dance with death began again. The angioplasty was speedily followed by the deterioration of her kidneys. With the onset of a new set of illnesses and the incessant battering her body received for nearly a decade, a distinct note of despondence and acceptance of the inevitable began to, uncharacteristically, house itself in Medha's mind.

Facing a slump in her spirits, Medha dwelt on the bad luck that dogged her all through 2008, spilling over into 2009. The really dangerous period was in December 2007, when she was at death's door again.

A massive kidney failure had led to her collapse and it was a struggle to keep her alive. She was in the ICU at Hinduja Hospital for 15 days and the New Year was brought in at the hospital.

After her angioplasty in November at Mount Sinai, fed up of her medical regimen, she had resisted going into the hospital again. Perhaps if Medha had checked into a hospital in Mumbai a couple of weeks earlier, the near-death crisis could have been averted. And when she finally did go to the hospital, it was not for the critical condition of her kidneys but for an intense stomach infection contracted after a *chaat* (Indian street food) session.

A virulent bout of food poisoning and diarrhoea had forced her to head to Hinduja Hospital on December 18, 2007. Anup was travelling, so she went to the hospital with a friend.

She had gone there because of the stomach infection but it was her failing kidneys that felled her. And she fainted at the hospital.

Once the doctors wheeled her into the ICU, she blanked out. "I didn't remember anything after that," Medha said, bewildered that one whole week of her life had vanished. She was in such a critical condition that her mother and sisters flew down, fearing the worst again.

Medha had a memory lapse about it, all those crucial days were erased like a blackboard wiped clean. "I don't remember any of it. I don't remember my sisters coming down, I don't remember anything. I only know that when I woke up, my mother and my elder sister were there and my younger sister called me up and asked, 'Hey, why were you not answering me properly when I came to see you?' I couldn't even recall that she had been there with me. I don't know where those days just vanished."

Medha's sisters were aghast to find Anup away for a show at such a crucial juncture. 'But she's going to be all right,' he had replied with standard calmness. It was difficult for anybody else to share his optimism at that moment.

Medha's memory returned only after she came out of the crisis alive but with her kidneys severely damaged. "When I came out, the doctors were still trying to save my kidneys. They didn't want to put me on dialysis just yet, so they put me on diuretics. I pulled on with them until April 2008, when I went to the US again."

A biopsy revealed that her kidneys were in a very bad condition. "I saw the nephrologist and the heart specialist there and they insisted that I be put on dialysis immediately because it had started to affect my heart. And so, on April 23, 2008, I went on dialysis for the first time."

With her heart threatening to go into rejection because of kidney failure, a three-times-a-week dialysis routine became mandatory. With it came Medha's first real bad case of plummeting morale which lasted all through 2008, culminating in another life-sapping crisis on the festive day of Diwali.

She spoke dispiritedly, perhaps for the first time ever. "My social pattern has changed. I am not always well, I get tired easily. We only go to parties hosted by people really close to us. We go early and come back early.

"I may look well but the truth is, there are certain aspects of the dialysis that I am not taking to very well. I keep getting fever after every dialysis which is very exhausting. The only way out for me is to opt for a kidney transplant. Otherwise, I will have to be on dialysis all my life."

The thought that had never surfaced during her heart transplant took refuge in her mind – Medha began to go under, like the inevitable was standing before her. The ebullience and the strong mental strength to keep battling every odd thrown at her, was slowly beginning to ebb.

"I am living on borrowed time," she accepted with resignation. "If we didn't have the money, I wouldn't be alive today.

"What I must mention here is that one of the people who helped us with money was Shekhar (Kapur). At that time he had told us not to mention it to anybody but he was very gracious about it. He told me that he owed it to me because he had made me put money in unprofitable businesses. Though we paid back every rupee, it was really nice of an ex-husband to help out at a critical time like that."

Medha also understood that she was extremely privileged to afford such a financially depleting medical treatment. Reality would stare her in the face every time she went for dialysis and saw the fragile position of other patients.

"The people who come for dialysis hail from a humble background," she observed. "While I use my dialyser once and throw it away, they are so desperate that they use it 15 or 20 times. I use an advanced dialyser which is imported from the US. They see me discard it each time and can't believe it. Once, a shrivelled old Gujarati lady asked me, 'Can't I wash and re-use your dialyser?' I do realise that I'm lucky to afford this illness."

Loyal Man Friday Ramchandra would go along with Medha for her tri-weekly dialysis. But counting your blessings could not take away from the ordeal of watching your body give way again and again.

"My mental state has been pretty bad," she said. "The fever that comes on after dialysis is an additional problem. I have been having niggling little problems all along. Somewhere along the way, I had gout.

"The doctors here said that my echocardiogram and my heart were so bad that I couldn't fly to the US. My echocardiogram was bad because of the kidney failure. My heart is better now since I started the dialysis but not as good as it was just after the transplant. There's something called ejection fraction to check how well your heart is pumping. That plummeted in December, 2007. But in July, 2008, it improved with dialysis.

"I have been keeping up my spirits all these years but lately, there have been too many medical setbacks and the future looks dim. So I have lost a bit of the positivity which I had during my heart transplant.

"There are times when I feel like giving up," she confessed to an unusual weakness. "It is exhausting to keep doing so many tests and invasive procedures, deal with doctors, make frequent trips to the hospital."

The doctors asked her to be prepared for another heart transplant or for both, heart and kidney transplants, putting her in a dilemma. She realised that if her heart was not strong enough, the kidney transplant would be a risky option. A kidney transplant would also entail more medication, ultimately leading to another kidney failure down the years. She wondered if her heart could withstand it all.

"Therefore, we are seriously thinking of alternatives which are not there. While a lot of research has been done on stem cells for the heart, spine, cancer and diabetes, not much work has been done on the kidney," she realised, adding to her newfound pessimism.

"My illness has become a full-time job," she stated in a dull, flat voice.

In 2008, with every new month, her mental strength steadily depleted and every new day found her vacillating between wanting a kidney transplant and cancelling the thought, willing to remain on dialysis for as long as she could.

Marvellously, what showed that she still had some of her old spunk was when she steadfastly refused to take anti-depression tablets. Although her doctors in New York and Mumbai and spiritual guru Deepak Chopra too, had recommended them, Medha never took recourse to those pills.

In 2008, in her rare period of despondence, when Medha began to look outside for inspiration, she found it in buoyant 76-year-old actor Shammi Kapoor.

"I have taken inspiration from Shammi Kapoor who said, 'On three days of the week I go for dialysis, the rest of the four days are mine, and I can do what I like with it.'" (Shammi Kapoor passed away three years later in 2011.)

"I am all right when I'm at home," she remarked. "Otherwise I tend to be a bit unsteady and I stagger on my feet. The problem is the fever that occurs after the dialysis. It shouldn't be happening."

Renal failure brings with it a whole host of complications and restrictions. Medha was allowed only 1,000 ml of water a day which included foods like *dal* (lentils) and juice. A low salt, high-protein diet was recommended, with two eggs and a piece of chicken or fish. Essentially not much of a meat-eater, she preferred to get her proteins from sprouts and cottage cheese. Fruits were a restricted item too, because of the water content in them. The limit on her intake of water also posed a problem when she had to swallow a whole lot of medicines.

Year 2008 was starkly different from 2001 when Medha needed a new heart. "During the heart transplant, I enjoyed myself in the hospital. I didn't have morbid thoughts. Now I'm older, I'm tired of the illnesses. Also, my sisters and my mother have grown older, there have been deaths in the family. I lost a very dear cousin and two of my brothers-in-law. Kirti's husband Ashok Parashar never came to meet me in New York during the transplant but he used to write such lovely, encouraging letters to me every week. He too, has passed away.

"My mother has grown older and changed. After Ashok died, she just clamped up and wouldn't speak. It was awful. Now that I am on dialysis I can't even go and meet her often, I have to be back every second day. She too, can't come here anymore. The last time she was here with me for a long time was in December 2007 when I had the kidney failure. She went back to Delhi, got a bout of pneumonia and never recovered. She is 83 years old now and too old to travel. I'm happy to see her detached now. I hope that happens to me too."

The defeated tone didn't augur well for Medha who still had a long fight ahead of her.

"But man lives on hope," she continued. "I am hoping that someone comes up with a breakthrough. I am so uncomfortable with this huge belly, it's like I'm permanently pregnant. If they don't tap me soon, I will have to go to the hospital. I'll need help, nursing and so on.

"I am carrying so much water, it's putting pressure on my heart, and it's putting pressure on my other organs as well. I would like to get the tapping done here in Mumbai but because all my levels are low, they are not doing it."

Tapping gave relief but was strenuous in its own way. "For tapping, they put a needle into your stomach under ultrasound to see where the water has collected in the abdominal cavity," explained Medha. "This water does not come out in urination or dialysis or in any other manner. It's stuck there, so the only way is to tap it out. They put a needle in, insert a tube and let the water fall out as much as they can safely without weakening you because along with the bad, the good stuff, like minerals, also gets washed out.

"It takes an hour or two depending on how much water is coming out and the speed at which it all comes out. It is painful only in the beginning when they put the needle in, although they give you a local anaesthesia. But it is not a pleasant procedure and you need to rest after it. I get knocked out the next day.

"Before the heart transplant I had 25 tappings, some here, some in the US, one in Delhi also. But my general health was better then. My health has deteriorated since then and I feel really *bimar* (unwell). Earlier, on non-dialysis days, I would go out for lunches, movies, meet friends. That has all come down quite drastically. On non-dialysis days too, I'm not fine anymore."

On World Heart Day in September, 2008, Medha's positivity further evaporated. Sounding beaten and tired, she said, "I was at Siddharth Kak's house a few days ago where some Pakistani singers had come over. The singers were so good that I was mesmerised but the next day I just crashed."

The mood continued all through the year between wanting the kidney transplant and not wanting to face another tiring surgery. Both her flesh and her spirit had become too weak to withstand another onslaught.

On the days that she resolved to go in for a kidney transplant, she would ramble, "I'm so fed up of dialysis. I'm dying to see the hills. I used to go at least three times a year to the Himalayas, now I can't even travel. The last time I went there was around May, 2007. We had gone to a very nice resort in Dharamshala called Glenmoor where the likes of Richard Gere stay when they come to meet the Dalai Lama. It's very serene and clean, with all the *suvidhas* (conveniences) like Wi-Fi, television, hot and cold water. It's about 9,000 ft above sea level. I can withstand the cold if I am well covered. Otherwise, by and large, I don't like the cold because my body is so utterly weak.

"I desperately need to go in for a kidney transplant but before that the fever has to be treated. Fever signifies an infection and surgery is dangerous when there's an infection in the body."

Meanwhile, the doctors were in no hurry to tap out the water from her stomach because the water retention by itself was not harming her. It was simply a physical discomfort that she had to endure. "Water retention occurs because it is a combination of the heart not doing too well and the kidneys not functioning properly. Before my heart transplant, it was only because of the heart but now it's also because of the kidneys. If I get my kidney transplant done, the longevity of my heart will go up. My lifestyle will be so much better," she thought aloud.

And then there were days when Medha would dismiss the transplant by saying, "It may be the most practical thing to do in the future but we have done a rethink on it. I am not going in for a kidney transplant right now."

She would explain, "I am mentally ready but I am not physically fit for a transplant because I am ailing, sick and weak. I am like one of those ageing actresses, looking frail and ill."

The yes-no oscillation continued.

10

An Anxious Family Notes The Change

2008 Mumbai/Delhi

She was slipping away so fast that Medha would spend evenings crying, calling up her mother and weeping over the phone. She even sent sister Eeda an SMS which alarmed her family in Delhi.

The only man who watched her condition deteriorate but was sure she would pull out of it was husband Anup. And despite her flagging morale, Medha's inner strength helped the healing process.

As cardiologist Dr Alok Chopra observed, "It is medically proven that the mind is strong enough to make you heal even when medical science has given up on you. Medha's is one such rare case."

In 2008, even rarer was the predicament of 14-year-old schoolboy, Aryaman Jalota who had his own little tale to tell. A bright, intelligent boy, Aryaman recorded his feelings:

"I was three or four years old when mom went to the US for a checkup and to research how she could help herself. Then I think I was five or six when she was really bad and went to the hospital. I didn't know anything at that time, I don't remember what I was told but I wasn't too worried because my *Bua* (paternal aunt) was here and she took good care of me. I was concentrating on my studies, so it didn't affect me too much. Besides, I was so young, I didn't really understand all that was happening. At that time, I was only in Senior KG. Teachers are always nice to you at that age whether your mom is ill or not, because we're just kids, one step ahead of babies. So it was fine.

"Now I understand that she has kidney failure, she's on dialysis, she's going to get a kidney transplant and that's very serious.

"But I don't cry. I don't feel lonely, I have stuff to do, I don't cry."

Did he feel bad that she was not like other mummies?

"I'm used to that, so it's okay."

What was not okay was the constant discussion that he should be sent to a boarding school. "I'm not looking forward to boarding. Home is better, boarding is pathetic," he grumbled.

He may have sounded grown up and in control but the little boy in him peered out when Aryaman said, "I remember going to see mom in the hospital when I was small. We had to wear masks and a hospital gown. That was fun. I was curious when I saw all the tubes and would ask what they were for."

Medha offered, "Actually he is so used to seeing those tubes that they don't bother him at all. He may not like them but he's not afraid of them."

Was Aryaman ever afraid of losing his mom? Your heart went out to the little boy because it was a thought that had indeed crossed his mind and he had told himself how to deal with it.

"The thought has struck me," he nodded, "but mom is very strong and she's holding on to life. I am afraid because I love her a lot. If that happens, I won't like it but I'll hang on, I'll try my best to hang on. I like to think positive, so I don't think about these things. Whatever happens, I am prepared. I'll take it."

But the tender years showed up again as he said, "She's a good mom, she doesn't scold or nag me." And then he turned to his mom and grinned, "You had better buy me an iPhone now!"

The mood continued as he disclosed, "Actually I like going to the US. Whenever mom goes for checkups, I go with her. We have friends and cousins. It's fun for me because I don't have to go for the checkups. For me it's a holiday."

While Medha's condition was never hidden from Aryaman, nobody sat him down and explained just how critical it could all turn out to be. "My dad hasn't talked to me about it but I understood what was happening because people talked about it," he said with the intuitiveness of a child. "Like when some people tell me, you are a very brave child, I understand how serious it is."

He knew, for instance, that his mother was so critical in December 2007, that he could have even lost her. "But I am so engrossed in other things that I don't think about it."

Medha remarked, "Aryaman gets easily out of it. Even when I'm really ill, once I regain consciousness and speak to him, he's fine. Being an only child, he is used to finding things to keep himself busy. Both my husband and I are very independent; he has our genes."

Her son nodded, "I watch movies, I go on the computer, hang out with friends and I love video games."

14 years was no age to turn philosophical. As Anup put it, "We need Medha in our lives. Aryaman needs his mother."

Enough reason for Medha to defy death again and again.

"I do know that Medha wants Aryaman to become an adult before anything happens to her, so that he's able to handle himself. Hopefully that will make her live a little longer and I think that is what gives her the strength to fight on," disclosed Eeda.

But in 2008, watching Medha ebb day by day, this was one anxious family that knew that the dreaded sword could drop any time.

Yet, in this essentially no-high-drama family, right from Vimla and Anup to Aryaman and his aunts, the worry was never manifest in the wringing of hands or loud sobs and chest beating.

"I have never spoken to Medha as to how it feels (to be staring death in the face) on a day-to-day basis," admitted Eeda quietly. "Somehow I feel if I touch on the topic, it would be like suggesting something negative. I don't feel comfortable having that frank a chat with her."

It was also a straight-talking family that did not need crutches to see itself through a crisis. "No, we don't use crutches," agreed Kushla. "Touch wood, that way we have been a very strong family. We have also been through a lot with mummy. We have lost my dad, my sister, my husband, Kirti's husband."

Medha too, had personally gone through a failed marriage, blocked tubes and a late pregnancy. And just when she had settled comfortably into marriage and motherhood, her health deserted her.

"She has been very brave through it all, very practical in a lot of things," commented Kushla. "For this I would also give a lot of credit to Anup. He is very calm and his '*sab theek hoga, sab theek hoga,* she'll be fine' line has been almost a chant for him."

The one complaint Kushla sometimes nursed against Anup was that he was too often away from Medha, especially since her spirits tended to slump in his absence, perking up visibly when he was around.

"But Medha herself points out to me that he keeps working to be able to pay for what has been happening to her," continued Kushla. "Then one keeps quiet, one realises that he is doing it for her and for his son. Medha is so positive when Anup is around. He is always very supportive and very strong."

Medha acknowledged her husband's strength in the face of adversity as she remarked, "Anupji has been so good through my entire illness. I don't know if he is ever irritated. He is so ungrudging, I am really fortunate. He is ready to do anything for me and he is always there for me. When he goes away for a long spell, I feel it's a good break for him because he doesn't have to see an ill wife all the time.

"I feel bad that this problem has been dumped on him but he doesn't see it as one. He takes it as something that has to be done. When he is in town, he comes with me for blood tests, for doctors' meetings, drops me off for dialysis.

"Luckily, I'm not a whiney patient though recently I find myself getting to be one because I'm just so uncomfortable and tired. But generally speaking, I believe if you are in pain, you don't need to be a pain."

Medha cited her husband as an example to negate the general tendency of husbands who use their busy schedule as an excuse for not being available for the family.

"Husbands who say they don't have time are lying," she stated. "Nobody can be as busy as Anupji, he travels so much. Once a month to the US, once a month to some other country, like today he is in Holland. He will come back and go to Bangalore. But in between, he still gives me time, he gives Aryaman time, he makes time for the dog too. He also makes up for some of the things that I have stopped looking at now. Although we have trained staff who have been with us for a long time, when something at home is cracking or is rickety, he takes care of it."

Kushla observed, "Anup and Medha are very lovey-dovey. Even in public, they hold hands, they are very demonstrative. He is nice and gentle with her."

Medha had a favourite line about the love they share. Said she, "Love grows when you spend more time together, not in separation as it's romanticised. I found love in the sorrows life gave me. I strongly believe in caring deeply for one another and that's why we have always smiled when everything was crying in my life. This is the strength of togetherness."

The older sister in her made Kushla superstitious about the evil eye as she said, "Medha has had it very rough. I don't know if one believes in it but *usko nazar lag gaya hai* (someone has cast an evil eye on her). Even through her illness or when she had a bloated tummy, she looked so good. It's only now that she has started getting dark circles under her eyes and her skin is turning greyish. I am so scared of *nazar* (evil eye) that I just never pay her a compliment. If she asks me how she is looking, the best I say is, 'You're looking very nice.' I have told her that I don't pay her any compliments because I'm scared of nazar."

The family members may have given one another strength but there were moments of weakness when one of them quietly turned to a *tantrik* (spiritual healer) for direction.

Kushla didn't believe in any kind of mumbo-jumbo but before the transplant, she had gone to a guruji she had heard about. "Medha had gone to Columbia, Kirti was with her, when my cousin told me about a guruji on MG Road in Delhi that everybody was swearing by as a miracle worker. I was ready to try anything that would help Medha recover without a transplant.

"That guruji is no more. He used to wear a long, embroidered organza *choga* (loose garment) and was very popular. Several ministers, generals and brigadiers from the army were his followers.

"He was Punjabi. When I entered, he said, '*Ay dekho, Anup Jalota di saali*' (look, here's Anup Jalota's sister-in-law).

"He asked me to come back the next day with five kilos of *gur* (jaggery). I returned with my sister-in-law (husband's cousin) the following day with the *gur*. We were told to leave it outside and we went in. Then he asked my sister-in-law her husband's name and when she said, 'Vijay,' he said, 'Very good Vijay, good man.' So he knew something, he had some power.

"There were many people who believed in him. Journalist-turned-politician Arun Shourie's wife, who had a debilitating illness from a very early age and was in a wheelchair, was holding his hand and walking around. He had cured her to that extent.

"He blessed Medha's photograph and the *gur* and asked us to offer it at a Hanuman *mandir* (temple) before 12 noon. We did that. Then he told us that on Baisakhi, there would be a mela at the mandir. We went to that too but after that, I didn't really meet him.

"I don't believe in sooth-sayers, astrologers or tarot card readers. But I think Eeda might have gone to a tarot card reader though she doesn't believe in all this either."

Eeda did more than that. She disclosed, "A friend of mine who follows Art Of Living and is Sri Sri Ravi Shankar's disciple, was having a function at home. I asked Medha if she wanted me to ask Sri Sri Ravi Shankar anything and she said, 'Yes, please ask him, what do you do when you want to fight your condition but however strong your mind may be, your body won't allow you to because it keeps reminding you that it's sick?'

"It was the second time I was seeing Sri Sri Ravi Shankar. I had met him the first time through the same friend when Medha had been diagnosed with cardiomyopathy. At that time, he had told me, 'Tell her to keep chanting Shivji's name.' The second time I met him and asked him Medha's question, he just said, 'Tell her she has to distract herself, keep her mind busy.'" There ended Eeda's tryst with a godman and it was largely left to Medha to heal herself.

"My respect for Medha has gone up tremendously, especially in the last one year, because you need to feel some sense of well-being from inside to be able to deal with this kind of illness. In the last one year, her health has been really plummeting but she does not give up," observed Eeda.

Anup too, had his share of believing in the supernatural owing to Medha's deteriorating condition. "*Bahut kiya hai, abhi tak chal raha hai* (I have done it all and continue to do so)," admitted Anup. "A week-long havan was performed in Nagpur. Wearing certain stones, gems, pujas...we have done it all. I was told to go to the *kabrastan* (graveyard) and give a certain amount of mutton to the *jallaad* (person who handles the funerary rites). I have done even that."

In discussing Medha's fight for survival and the change that had lately come over her, you needed to first understand the kind of person she was vis-à-vis other people.

Culled from those closest to her, the portrait of an extrovert emerged – a bright, spunky young lady used to getting attention and getting her way most of the time, eager to live life to the fullest. In this was also an element of self-absorption, which in hindsight perhaps helped her focus unwaveringly on, 'I, me, myself – and this is how I will survive.'

When younger sister Eeda's first marriage had crumbled from the word go, had Medha rallied around her as an older sister? "She had come and spent some time with me to guide me through it but she couldn't handle it," Eeda explained. "Medha never had the patience or the emotional strength to handle other people's issues. That's the way I felt about her."

Something happened between the sisters when Eeda was at an emotional low. "Medha was going to the US for a holiday. I was in London (with her first husband) and she came to stay with me for a couple of weeks," Eeda unspooled, without malice.

"I was going through a really bad time in that marriage and I decided to come back to Delhi for a while. So Medha ended up having to spend a couple of days with my ex-husband because she couldn't change her ticket or something like that. I don't think she could forgive me for it but it wasn't as if I had asked her to come and then abandoned her."

When Eeda's perspective of the incident was conveyed to Medha, she had a simple explanation for it: she had not paid a social visit to Eeda en route to the US. She had been specifically asked by the family to go and see if she could help Eeda patch up with her husband and thus save their marriage.

The London incident apart, Eeda had given a lot of thought to her older sister's nature and discussed another trait of hers which showed that Medha usually got life on her terms. She remarked, "You cannot talk to Medha about something that she does not want to discuss.

"Medha has always been very demanding, and to a great extent, she has always had her way," Eeda made a verbal character sketch of her sibling. "Not necessarily materialistically but in terms of time and attention. She is used to getting her way, used to attention, to people talking about her.

"Around the transplant time, she must have had insecurities of her own. Post-transplant, the steroids are supposed to affect you and she had become fairly aggressive and short-tempered. She did not have the patience to listen to you.

"After the surgery, she didn't want to be left alone even for a minute. There were times when she would be incorrigibly difficult. She couldn't see another person's point of view. I think she felt that her time was so precious, she didn't want it interfered upon by anything that she didn't desire. So, at times, that kind of attitude became a little difficult for other people to accept."

This crucial juncture was the time to pause and look at life's positives. At the end of an exhausting journey, one knew that Medha had found an almost inexhaustible source of mental strength to fight for her life. A source that may have depleted in 2008 but miraculously kept replenishing itself at all other times. Her family was the dream support system every patient needed to battle death-defying odds. But was Medha ever there for others?

"I can only talk for myself," replied Eeda. "Whenever I had a fiasco, she would drop everything and come. The only time she was not very equal to it was when there was that episode in London." But Medha's side of the London episode too, was an instance of how she had actually gone out of her way to see if she could help Eeda with her troubled marriage.

Unaware, Eeda continued, "Whatever was considered a negative quality in her has, touch wood, turned out to be positive for her."

That Medha also reciprocated her family's concerns for her was exemplified by one of Eeda's stray thoughts. Said Eeda, "One day I was talking to Medha on the phone when I mentioned something that had been on my mind. It was something that I couldn't talk about to my friends and I didn't want to disturb my mother with my problems. Medha's response to it was, 'You should know that you can talk to me at any time about anything that's bothering you. Just because I have my problems, don't think that you can't talk to me about yours. You can really talk to me, I'm still here.' That felt really nice.

"This real big change that has come into her," Eeda analysed, "is like surrendering to a situation. She has become a very calm person unlike what she used to be even five years ago. But it is scary too, because we don't want her to give up the fight."

It is an anxiety that Dr Alok Chopra also expressed. In October, 2008, he voiced his fear that this time he wasn't sure if Medha had the strength to cope with the crisis.

"We all are," affirmed Eeda. "But Medha continues to have her moments of strength. The other day I was talking to Radhika (Anup's cousin in New York) and she said that Medha now seemed open to the idea of another transplant."

It was simply yet another instance of Medha's indecisiveness over wanting to give life another shot and being overwhelmed with tiredness.

Eeda said reflectively, "Medha called me two days ago and said that the doctors had told her that if her heart was fine, she should get herself listed for a kidney transplant. For us that held out hope, it meant that the doctors felt there might be a chance of the heart being fine. It is such a touch-and-go situation. And if we are going through such myriad feelings, what must she be going through? What must Anup be facing, or Aryaman?'

Along with Medha, Eeda too had mellowed and she saw the change in herself when she said, "My whole attitude towards

Medha has also changed. Earlier, whenever I would go to Mumbai, I would always want to go out. But the last few times, I wanted to be at home and hang out with her."

Was this because there was a feeling that time might be running out for Medha?

"We have never talked about it," stressed Eeda. "Medha who was always a very strong fighter has become a very vulnerable person. If I ask her, what's up, the one phrase I hear a lot from her these days is, *'Bas aise hi hai'* (it's the same as before) and I don't know what to make of it. She never used to say that before."

The *'Bas aise hi hai'* attitude was a disturbing contrast to her usual spunk, evident even in May-June 2008, when she was in Delhi to get her dialysis done there. Mother Vimla remarked, "She was full of life even then. After dialysis too, she used to be up and about the next day."

"No, she would be fine the same day itself," Kushla recalled. "Medha had told me that since she felt much better after dialysis, we could go to Select City Mall which is close to the hospital and walk around for an hour or so before returning home.

"But that day, she wasn't feeling well after dialysis. I think it was the first time the post-dialysis fever came on. It was never there in Mumbai."

The fever after dialysis was the starting point of a sharp decline both in her health and in her will to bash on regardless.

It was chilling when Medha blandly announced that she was living on borrowed time.

"She is, we all know it," accepted Eeda. "Every time something happens to her, all of us start reading up on it. When she started getting this fever, I searched the net for 'fever after dialysis in the transplanted'. I spent hours looking it up and finally found one article on a Japanese woman who had gone through this kind of fever. After living with it for two years, they had found that it had something to do with the tube they used for dialysis. Once they changed the tube, her fever disappeared. So I quickly sent Medha a text message about it. The doctors tried it but it didn't work."

She was on the brink of going under so many times that Medha's family learnt to live with the fear of losing her. Eeda described the potpourri of emotions that the close members of a family encounter when one among them faces a fate as dire as this.

"It's a fear we all have," Eeda nodded. "When her kidneys collapsed in December, 2007, Anup was not in Mumbai and her friends called us up. By the time I reached there, I heard that my mom and sisters were also coming and I wondered what had happened. My mind just froze."

When sodium levels go down, there is usually some amount of disorientation in a patient. It happened to Medha and once she came out of it, the next 48 hours were critical. "The second day, she was in a trance-like situation, she just kept saying, 'Mama, Mama,'" recalled Eeda. "Medha doesn't remember those two or three days at all. That was one more time when we thought we were going to lose her. One has been living with that for 6-7 years now. Unfortunately, when the doctors at Mayo gave up on her, she was in a critical condition as her stomach was filling up every few days. They would tap out one to two litres each time."

The thought that they could lose Medha was something the family never sat and discussed in so many words. "Right now, I am talking about it dispassionately," Eeda deliberated. "When something goes on for a long time, I think your own defence mechanism doesn't allow you to keep up that emotional level.

Yet there are times like when I got a really desperate SMS from Medha. I was in my mother's room when I received it and I didn't know how to stay calm but I did. The SMS was literally like a plea saying, 'What do I do? Whatever I do is just failing.' I went home, called up my friend and cried to her. There was nothing else I could do.

"I oscillate between emotions," admitted Eeda. "In December, 2007, I felt very dejected. A lot of times I felt very guilty about telling her that I was going out of town or out for dinner. Even if I didn't tell her, I would feel guilty though I know she wouldn't mind my having a good time. I also know that this guilt trip is another common emotion one goes through in such situations.

"We all know that life does not stop, you need to keep going. You can't give up living but you can't help feeling guilty about it either, especially when you know that she wants so much to live."

Eeda watched her ageing mother cope with it differently. "When I lost my brother-in-law, Ashok, my mother just clammed up. If she has somewhat disconnected herself from what's going on, we all feel it's good for her. Like when she lost her youngest sister very unexpectedly, I thought my mother would be shattered. She cried but not to the extent that we thought she would."

Tani, who was as close as a sibling, also found Medha sometimes on the verge of switching off. "This time I find her spirits sagging a bit. She would say, '*Kuch bhi le lo mere se* (take anything from me) but give me my husband, my child, my health, just for a little while longer."

It was like she wanted her health on loan from Fate until she was ready to call it a day.

From her doctor to her family and friends, there was anxiety writ large in 2008. Almost everybody echoed the same thought as Kushla, who said, "I'm afraid for her. Now I'm anxious all the time because she is really very seriously ill. We can only keep hoping that she gets better."

It was a solo performance by Anup who alone continued to be adamant that Medha would overcome this crisis too, and that he would bring her back home again. "He was not scared when her valve problem cropped up, or when Mayo accidentally botched up her case," remarked Kushla. "Even during the heart transplant, he stood calmly by her side. But the rest of us are all scared right now. Since December 2007, it has been very scary."

On the days that Medha's will took a beating, she invariably turned to one of her sisters. "When I was in Toronto with my daughter," Kushla shared, "she called me up and cried for half-an-hour. She was saying, 'I'm very tired, I don't want to live anymore. I can't fight it, *bahut ho gaya* (it has gone on for too long).' And I kept telling her, 'What nonsense, Aryaman still needs you, you have to keep fighting.' What else could one say? You couldn't say, you will be all right, because we all know that she can't be completely back to normal. But even if she is 60 to 70 per cent all right, it will be good for her."

Eeda was intensely emotional about the many changes that she saw in Medha over the years. After 9/11, when she had walked into Medha's room at the hospital before the transplant, she had walked out practically inconsolable. "From looking healthy and having a big stomach (with the fluid accumulation that needed tapping), suddenly she was all shrivelled up. She had also cut her hair short and I wasn't prepared to see her look like that," Eeda described her reaction.

"Again, in September 2008, I met her twice and within two weeks, her health had really gone down. A greyish pallor had settled on her face and she was once again looking very shrivelled. I could see that she wanted to fight it but was unable to."

On October 8, 2008, Eeda got an SMS from a dishearteningly demoralised Medha, a Medha so exhausted that she was clearly going under. The close sisterly exchange of messages disturbed Eeda so thoroughly that she hid it from their ageing mother. But she had the following exchange saved on her mobile phone:

Medha*: Mama, mama, I'm always feeling cold. Mama, mama, make me a little bold. I cannot take this anymore, my whole body is sore. Where's the God you promised, who would cuddle me and hold?*

Eeda*: You getting poetic, good! Close eyes and hug yourself. The God inside will hug you.*

Medha*: The God inside me fled, and cruelly left me while I bled. Who will hug me now? How can I go on, how?*

Eeda*: Your family, your sister will hold and hug you, in the* 'bister' *(bed)* ☺☺

Could Medha's failing health have been controlled, could any of it have been stemmed before such a sharp deterioration? Eeda was the only person who mentioned that perhaps Medha should never have returned to India after her transplant. If she had stayed on in the US, her health may not have plummeted the way it did in 2008.

"Her kidneys started going bad in October-November, 2007 when she went to New York for treatment. She had gone there for her kidney but they put a stent in her heart. They forgot about the kidney and started looking only at the heart angle. When she came back, she had a complete kidney failure in December. All that may not have happened had she been there all along."

Relocating to the US after her heart transplant in 2001 was a move that Medha and Anup had seriously considered.

Medha revealed, "After the heart transplant, Dr Gass and others had suggested that we move to the US. Now that I literally had an American heart, they said that we could get citizenship. They didn't want their good work to go wrong and told me, 'We have spent a heart on you and we want you to live.'

"Between ourselves, we seriously discussed it. Anupji said he could relocate to any part of the world as long as flights were easily available. He had always nursed the idea of opening devotional music schools in the US and he has opened one already. So there was a lot he could do there with the kind of diaspora that we now have in the US."

However, Medha longed to be home and she was keen that Aryaman be brought up in their homeland. "Anupji and I both love India, this is our home." Besides, Medha was too exhausted to welcome the thought of doing everything herself with no staff around.

The comfort of home worked well for more than five years. In fact, after researching on the net, on the fifth anniversary of her heart transplant, she sent Eeda and many other people an e-mail that said, 'Normally there are very few transplants which do well up to five years. I seem to have crossed that.' The big sigh of relief was barely exhaled when, a few months later, her kidneys emitted red signals which snowballed into the crisis that almost took her life in October, 2008.

Eeda rued that while during the transplant there was room for optimism, in 2008 nobody had a clue how to halt the progressively deteriorating situation.

Medha was so critical that Anup flew her out in October, 2008.

Anup replayed the trauma of Medha's fourth date with death. "On Diwali day (2008), we were together in New York at night when her fever shot up to 103.9°. She couldn't talk, she couldn't sit up, and she was in great pain. With great difficulty, I somehow got her from the hotel room to the hospital as an emergency case. She spent the better part of the next two months in the ICU."

The weakness turned her helpless; she wanted to succumb and stop the struggle.

"For the first time, Medha herself told me, 'Let me go, I can't take it anymore'," Anup described her distress. "She was in great pain and said to me, 'I can't bear it, let me go, stop doing so much for me.' But I said, 'No, we're going to fight it, I am going to bring you back.'"

He did. The doctors tracked the infection that was bringing on the fever after dialysis and corrective treatment followed. Slowly, she could walk a bit, holding on to some support.

Dr Gass couldn't believe the figure before him. "When I saw Medha in January 2009, after years, I almost yelled at her. She was almost a shell of her former self. Physically, and also in her eyes, I could see that she did not have the will to live anymore. She was being dragged along, she was not standing up. I told her, 'You have to pick yourself up, you have to eat better.' Do yoga, imagery, do whatever it takes to get better. Then (later in the year) she started doing really well."

"We were very fortunate to have brought her back alive for the fourth time," Anup acknowledged it as a blessing from above.

Meanwhile, a kidney donor had come forward.

SAVOY

Ominous outing – Mussoorie, 2000, where it all began

Sunita by my side – in Mussoorie

We sing and play together – Bina-Talat Aziz, Medha-Anup, Pankaj-Farida Udhas

Stairway to positivity – before surgery

Positively united – daughters Kushla and Kirti flank mom Vimla; (behind) Eeda and Medha, and sons-in-law Vikram, Anup and Ashok

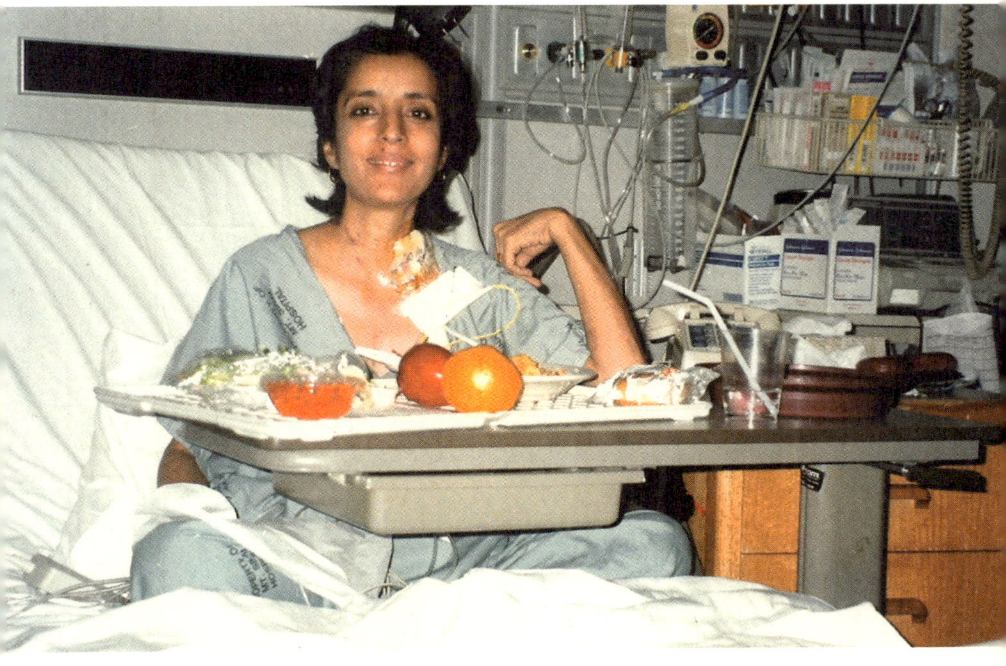

Give me a heart – in NY hospital before the transplant

Not without Radhika – the support system in NY

Genes of steel – with father-in-law Purushottam Das Jalota

Hale and hearty – quite literally, in NY

Back to normalcy – Medha in NY post-transplant

Rappelling before grappling with another disease –
active in Goa five years post-transplant

Thanks, Dr Gass – Medha glows five years post-transplant

Picture of health – Anup, Medha and Aryaman on Dr Vimla Gujral's 80th birthday

Hearty 50th – Ila Arun, Shabana Azmi, Nandita Puri,
Neena Gupta and the birthday girl

Music is the food of love – Medha with guru Pandit Jasraj

The maestro's stroke – with MF Hussain on his last birthday in London

India's most famous – with former Prime Minister Atal Bihari Vajpayee

Bonding with a neighbour – with ghazal singer Ghulam Ali

Love conquers it all – Medha and Anup

11

The Magic Returns

Mumbai, 2009

January opened a new chapter on the miracles that can be wrought with optimism and will power. For someone who had given a scare even to doctors who had known her for more than two decades, the gaunt, grey-skinned patient in a wheelchair proved to be a marvel worth close scrutiny by medical science.

Four months after she had cried out asking her husband to let her go, Medha weighed a light 43 kilos. But back to her cheerful self, Medha chirped happily, "When talking to you last year, I remember I was very depressed because I couldn't see any silver lining. I think I started regaining my health once the fever went away."

Detecting the cause of the fever before treating it took its time.

"On October 20, Diwali day, I got admitted to a hospital in New York and came out two months later. They did a lot of tests, pricked and cut my body but finally found the infection and treated me for it. The fever, which was occurring due to a very rare sort of infection in my abdomen area, vanished after that. After I came out of the hospital, I stayed in New York for one more month and returned end-January, 2009.

"A less intense version of the fever recurred in March which was treated with the same medicine that I was given in New York. I went to the US again in April for 15 days for a regular checkup, just to ensure that everything was going right and the doctors there thought I had recovered quite well from the last time they had seen me.

"I was in a really bad shape when I returned from the US in January. I was too scared to come back to India, looking the way I did. I was extremely weak, my face had turned black and I had lost a lot of weight. In three-four months, I have turned around but some problem or the other keeps cropping up with the dialysis. I have a hernia which keeps popping out of my belly. Vertigo is also a new problem.

"We now have a donor from Anupji's family for the kidney transplant. The match is good here but it has to be tested in the US where I will have the transplant. If I gain enough in terms of weight and health, we can go for it later this year."

The patient who had wanted to give up the battle for life had vanished. "Yes, I am back to being in a positive frame of mind," she laughed. "Last year, I was really down and out. When I went to the US (October, 2008), I was really ill. Within two days, Anupji had to take me to the emergency ward where I collapsed. The following two months in the hospital were really bad. My morale was at its lowest and I was even ready to give up the fight."

Medha had hallucinations around her hospital room. One day, she found it had turned into a Japanese room, another day, there was a tea party going on and yet another day, she was screaming, "There is a lizard in my room, chase it away!" From that frail and fragile condition to normalcy and sanity was a long and tiring but successful journey.

Much improved, a new problem was the vertigo which she hoped would play itself out in a while. "I just have to live it out," she accepted.

There was also the hernia which the doctors did not want to treat surgically. "They don't consider it a great problem. It's not painful but it's irritating and it pops out of my clothes which is a real nuisance," she remarked.

Mentally prepared for a kidney transplant, she knew that if it did not happen, she would have to be on dialysis forever. She kept count of the many ailments and said, "My heart is okay at the moment. Nothing can be done about the additional vascular disease, so I'll just have to live with it. My energies are a little low because of that. Dialysis weakens you a lot and makes you lose weight. A kidney transplant will rejuvenate me and help my heart stay healthy. It will also make a very big difference to my lifestyle. I will not have to go three times a week to the hospital for dialysis, each time for four-five hours. With dialysis, the blood pressure drops, there is dehydration. But at least it keeps you alive and it keeps your kidneys functioning.

"It is true that last year I nearly gave up," she giggled at the dramatic memory. "But Anupji and all the others got me out of that mode. Radhika and Ashokbhai in New York did so much *seva* (service) for me. Radhika has been like one big angel. She would massage my legs, sometimes even clean me up when I couldn't get up to go to the bathroom. Who would do that?

"After the infection was treated, they could not discharge me because I was so weak. When I was slightly better, I went to Radhika's house in December, 2008, recuperated there and came back to India on January 20, 2009. I gained strength in

February and March and lost a bit of it because of the recurring infection for which I was once again hospitalised at Hinduja."

Medha was no fool. If she confidently faced the inevitable and returned alive each time, it was with the full knowledge that her life could be snuffed out any moment, any day. "When I think of death, I try to convince myself that I am in transit. Isn't that what the *Gita* says?" she queried. "I try not to be afraid of impermanence."

Not afraid but wiser after so many visits to doctors and hospitals, Medha and Anup certainly learnt how the medical fraternity worked. "For patients like me who have been so chronically ill, I have discovered that the hospitals make you do a lot of tests that you may not need," she expounded. "I found this true of the US as well as India. They made me do a PET scan in India. They have state-of-the-art machines and methods but they have no trained staff to read and interpret the reports! The reports we were given were so vague that we wondered why we were asked to do this ₹ 25,000 test in the first place."

Her three-month stint in the US was no better. "October, November and December of 2008 were really bad. In order to find the infection, the hospital did a whole lot of unnecessary tests during the two months that I was hospitalised.

"Finally, when they found the infection, the treatment was so strong that it took me two to three months to get my body in order. When I came back to India in January, 2009, I was frail, weak and in the doctor's words, malnourished. I looked like a famine-struck refugee."

One of the many major factors that came together to keep Medha alive was finding Dr Gass who had presided over her heart transplant in 2001. Her best medical advisor so far, one of the points on Dr Gass' must-do list was to continue with yoga, reiki and meditation. He believed that the ultimate well-being of a patient lay in therapeutic alternatives.

Medha also had two meetings in New York with internationally renowned spiritual guru, Deepak Chopra. The notoriously busy guru found time for her only because of his friendship with Shekhar Kapur. It was the latter who facilitated the meetings.

"The first time I met Deepak Chopra, he asked me to try and meet him once more before leaving New York. His secretary gave me an appointment one week later. Simple, gentle and soft, he asked me to meditate, showed me methods of doing it and helped me get set for it. I have been doing it sporadically but I have been doing it."

The encounter with Deepak Chopra also left Medha vastly amused. "He has a shop-cum-spa-cum-little meeting room in New York, near Broadway. He sits in a tiny little room with just one seat for him and another for someone else to sit on. He is a short, simple personality but he had these really crazy red shoes and dramatic, punky glasses. What I liked about him was what he said: 'What am I telling people? I am only reiterating what is already written in our *Upanishads*, in our *Rig Veda*, in all our ancient texts and scriptures. I haven't invented any of it. I am only re-arranging it.' I liked it very much that he was admitting that whatever he was teaching the world was what had already been written hundreds of years ago."

Medha progressed so well that she flew to Delhi in June 2009 to spend her birthday with her mother and sisters. On July 29, she hosted a huge, lavish *qawwali* (form of Sufi devotional music) programme to celebrate Anup's 56th birthday. She attended parties, book launches and concerts, and got herself a swank new haircut from her personal stylist in Versova. She had psyched herself into believing that the kidney transplant would be her next gift from the gods. If ever a patient was ready for her next surgery, it was this full-of-beans Medha.

She practically gurgled, "Anupji's cousin, Rajesh Jalota who lives in Lucknow, has very graciously and very kindly offered his kidney to me. In India people are unfortunately so bound by superstition and religion that they don't donate organs even of the dead, leave alone living organs like the kidney. I feel that donating an organ from your body to save another person's life, is the biggest sacrifice anyone can make for another."

The imminent trip abroad to get a new kidney fitted had already infused new zest into Medha and she responded with the spirit of an inveterate fighter once the agenda had been set. Now that a donor had been sourced and the doctors in the US were awaiting her arrival, the next item to be ticked off was a kidney transplant. With her programme for the next few months clearly spelt out, Medha was once again in peak form, ready for the battle.

"I am feeling very good," she sparkled. "I'm going to be away for two months or more, so I want to meet all my friends before I go. When I come back, I'm going to be a different person, a person who doesn't have to be on dialysis, a person free to travel, free to meet her friends again. Hopefully, I won't have to say, 'If it's Monday, it's dialysis day, I can't meet you.' I won't have to miss a concert or a play. I say 'hopefully' because I don't want to pump up my dreams too much," she added, levelling her joy with a touch of pragmatism.

"I am also very, very apprehensive and nervous because I know what a major surgery is all about. The stay in the hospital, being tested over and over again, getting pinched, poked and cut, the surgery, the anaesthesia, the disorientation when you come out of it, the stitches, the pain of the healing, the hair fall, adjusting the dosage of medication, trying to get your systems back to working order," she drew a list of what the ordeal entailed.

"The most important part of healing is when you can start going to the bathroom properly," she noted wisely. "That is when you are considered okay. To reach from surgery to that part is very painful. The post-surgery trauma is quite awful. I also don't take to anaesthesia too well. There is disorientation and I tend to hallucinate. Nevertheless, I am looking forward to it too," she put in cheerfully, "because if the surgery is successful, my life will change, it will be a real turnaround for me."

With the end to the ordeal almost in sight, it was time for Medha to put her personal mantra for life into words: "Faith can definitely heal.

"One of the reasons why I was in such a critical condition all through 2008, was because I was so mentally down that it manifested in my body. I don't know where the faith comes from but I have always looked at the happier side of life. If I can't go out, I start gardening at home. I don't mind if I have half a life. If I can't climb the mountains, going up to the foothills will be good enough for me."

Before she boarded her flight to New York, she sent a friend a flurry of text messages. One read: "My *toh* heart is fluttering. Even my dead kidneys must be feeling the throb of excitement!"

On November 27, 2009, a Jet Airways flight took off from Mumbai at 03.00 hours, with Medha and Anup on board, eagerly looking forward to coming home in the New Year with a new kidney, another lease of life and a fresh resolve to live life queen-size.

It turned out that we had all talked too soon. Four text messages sent by Medha, two from New York and two from Mumbai, told a story that was enough to burst any bubble of happiness.

On 01/12/09

Hello. My donor n I had major blood work yesterday. They took out 14 vials, 14 big vials of my blood! Will know where we stand next week. Will keep you posted. Love

On 09/12/09

Hi. Bad news. My kidney donor has been rejected. Not matching. So now I'll come back to India, search for another donor. And back to the grind of dialysis.

On 17/12/09

Am back. What a disappointing failure this whole mission was! I don't know now where to gather hope and energy from. All is *phus* (useless).

Same day, a few minutes later

I'm trying to accept this setback with grace. It's not easy tho I keep telling myself that it's for the better.

Only one thought prevailed on those watching Medha: could she survive such a devastating and demoralising setback?

12

Kidney Watch

Mumbai 2010

Medha softly sent up a wish. "Life is so full of magic. There's so much I yet wanna do. I want to tell the gods up there, let me fly a little more. I need more time."

She was back in town and back to dialysis three times a week. Putting behind her the dispiriting experience of going to New York only to have the donor kidney rejected, Medha skipped back into Page 3 again. But she perceptively remarked, "I'm very aware of my mortality and accordingly choose priorities. I have now become an energy-miser. I save energy for the more precious people and things in life."

In February, the doctors in the US rejected yet another donor – Medha's own sister, Eeda who was ready to give her a kidney. The Jalotas also explored the possibility of having a transplant done in Singapore where politician Amar Singh had got himself a fresh kidney. Medha, however, drew a blank again, as the Singaporeans were not as well-equipped by experience as their counterparts in New York to handle a second organ transplant on a heart-transplant patient. As her doctors in New York constantly reminded Medha, the kidney could keep functioning indefinitely with dialysis. It was her heart care that she could not afford to neglect.

The setbacks didn't rob the sunshine from her life as Medha put on a bit of weight and her battered body gradually began to show signs of health. Even as they awaited a donor whose kidney would be accepted by the surgeons, Anup and Medha were back to being the toast of the celebrity circuit.

Few realised that behind the sunny smile captured by photographers, stood a patient who needed a life-saving organ; a patient who had spent more than a decade in and out of hospitals and still had serious, unfinished business to reckon with; a patient who had seen close-ups of death not once or twice but four times; a woman who had more spirit and spunk than all the celebrity survivors featured in the glossies.

The golden words that fuelled her undying enthusiasm: Life is for living and my heart is still beating.

13

The Support System

The medical world has accepted that it is mind over matter that has kept Medha alive. There is increasing medical evidence and acceptance in the fraternity that there was something beyond the realm of medical science that brought Medha back from death's door, many times over. The reference was not to alternate therapies or spiritual gurus but to the strength of the mind that conquered bodily weakness. It was a theory best articulated by Dr Alok Chopra who had watched Medha both as a charmed family friend and as an alarmed cardiologist.

He first met Medha in her prime in Delhi. "I think I met Medha in relation to her elder sister's wedding," Dr Chopra strained to recollect. "My first impression of her was that she was an extremely good-looking girl and she had a very appealing, energetic sort of aura with a very nice smile. She was the sort of person you would want to go up and meet. She was very talkative, very vibrant. That first impression is still the same impression I have of her today."

It was a surprising remark coming from a doctor who had, time and again, seen her life almost ebbing away from her. In fact, Dr Alok Chopra had seen Medha through practically all the stages of her near-fatal illnesses.

"If I remember correctly, I first saw her professionally in the early '80s," he said. "That was when she had a swelling in her legs; there was a bluish discolouration in her legs. The murmur I had detected then was a chance finding. We had done an echocardiogram but at that time, it was not as sophisticated as it is today. The impression conveyed then was that there was some obstruction to the blood-flow in the valves leading from the heart to the lung. The heart muscle had appeared normal. We thought it was a congenital valve thickening but it was not a classical diagnosis that we could make, nor could we put a name to the illness. All we could do was to recommend a follow-up and see how it would go."

Alok rejected the general idea that Medha had a benign murmur in her heart. "It wasn't as if we thought it was completely benign," he countered. "We knew that there was something amiss which could progress. But she always seemed well and she was very active, singing, dancing and doing everything. She started to feel a little unwell only towards the late '90s, and it was only around 1999-2000 that we realised that what she had was a life-threatening problem. She had a serious rhythm disorder of the heart and it led to ventricular failure. Ventricular failure can cause a fall in blood pressure and many other things, and that's when we knew that there was something serious going on."

By the time the diagnosis came through, Medha had gone into critical heart failure. "When she did go into heart failure, we realised that this was a condition called cardiomyopathy which is a muscular disorder in the heart muscles and has an effect on the pumping capacity of the organ. It affects the different parts of the heart muscles asymmetrically. Most cardiomyopathies are classified under a clinical syndrome that emerges from each of those types. But in her case, it was very difficult to give it a specific name, which is why we thought she should go to the

US to find out the problem. We also realised that she needed a biopsy of the heart muscle to make a pathological diagnosis and thereby give it a name.

"In layman's terms, the heart has four chambers, two on the left and two on the right. The left chambers receive oxygenated blood from the lungs and the chambers on the right pump it back into the lungs. In her condition, the heart muscles had a disorder, a type of weakness which affected both the filling and the pumping. The chambers became big and this also affected the functioning of the valve. So it was all pretty complicated."

Just as the doctor's diagnosis sounded dire, he came up with an observation that had little to do with text book medical science. "The heart condition that Medha suffered from was actually not curable," he said. "It is possible that the disease becomes static or it burns out but it cannot reverse. It doesn't get better."

Yet, Medha not only got better and survived but she was also back on her feet. Her heart may have given way but with a strapping young heart transplanted into her body, Medha had new life pumped into her. Dr Alok clinically discussed the normal life expectancy of such a patient.

"With the availability of new technology, a heart-transplant patient now has about 80 per cent chance of being okay for about 5 to 10 years and the rest depends on her pre-morbid condition – that's her medical condition prior to surgery. There is no doubt that every patient reacts differently. Because you have to take some drugs to prevent rejection of the new heart, you do get coronary disease on the transplanted heart, which Medha actually got and she had to undergo angioplasty. All that took a toll on the heart. So it's difficult to say how long but there are people who have stayed alive for 15 to 20 years."

When Medha collapsed at the end of 2008 with kidney failure and recurring fever, Dr Chopra had been a very worried man who accepted that this time she was delicately poised between life and death.

Yet Medha came out of it again and she bounced back in 2009, surviving on tri-weekly dialysis. "She was truly in serious trouble then," explained Dr Chopra.

If Medha won that battle for life again, Alok traced it to reasons other than strictly medical. "Notwithstanding the support she got from her immediate family and her friends, I think the primary reason she has carried on is her intrinsic nature, which is wonderfully positive, and her extreme desire to live life to the fullest."

In 2010, Medha had even recovered from the trauma of going all the way to New York only to have the donor kidney rejected and come back to dialysis again. But Dr Chopra, who had started having faith in unexplained miracles, foresaw her fighting back.

"She's back to being her very positive self and I'm confident now that these miracles are possible. We have to just watch them happening. No doubt she is in a lot of trouble but at the moment I don't think any of us, and most of all Medha herself, are focusing on outcomes. We are focusing on the fact that we need to get better regardless of the outcome and we will take it as it comes."

If a hardcore medical man had begun to pin his faith in miracles after watching Medha almost perform them, then friends and family who had stood by, looked on with awe. Radhika Seth Tandon, Anup's cousin in New Jersey was wonderstruck and energised after closely observing Medha.

Roly-poly and robust, Radhika who is married to Mridul Tandon, a qualitative analyst with Wall Street, was one of those who stood vigil by Medha's bedside every time she was in New York, nursing her right through her heart transplant and again, when her kidneys failed. She became so familiar with Medha's hospital routine and her cheerful company that she was practically bursting with happiness when the Jalotas decided to go back to Dr Gass for the kidney transplant.

"What a personality Dr Gass has!" exclaimed Radhika. "Actually it's not just his personality but also the way he talks to a patient and makes them comfortable, which is truly amazing. I'm very glad that Medha is going back to Dr Gass."

Medha often mentioned the immense gratitude she felt for those who had helped her come out of her critical illnesses time and again. To be by Medha's bedside, Radhika, for instance, not only left behind two little kids in Mridul's care, she even ungrudgingly cleaned her mess when the patient was in a helpless condition. Medha often wondered, "Who does so much for anyone these days?"

It was an integral part of the miracle that so many hands stretched out to pick up Medha every time she was down. It was unquestionably because her people-friendly personality had helped her unwittingly create a strong bond with a wide variety of friends.

"I met Medha the first time in 1996," rewound Radhika. "My daughter is six months older than Aryaman and I named her after Medha. Strangely enough, I had been admiring Medha for the longest time, much before she and Anup got together, right from the time she was married to Shekhar. I didn't know her personally at that time, I only knew of her as a celebrity and I liked her personality. When she got married to Anup, I asked him, 'Are you sure it's the same Medha?' He assured me that she was the one and I was glad that I would finally get to meet her.

"When I came down from the US in 1996, I met her for the first time. It was at one of those family gatherings where you meet all your cousins. She was very sweet. I wanted to buy *bindi*s (dot on the forehead) and other things before going back home. Medha left both the kids (hers and mine) at home with the maid and drove me to Dadar to buy all my stuff. After that, every time I came down to Mumbai, we would have one family lunch where all of us would meet."

Medha's personality thus made a firm connection with one more person and Radhika rose to the occasion without a second thought when the crisis hit the Jalotas.

"In 2001, when she fell ill and had landed in Mayo, Anup *Bhai* (brother) and I were talking on the phone," recalled Radhika. "He had a programme for three days and he mentioned that Medha would be alone. I said, 'Why would she be alone?' I had my second baby, Maanya, by then, who was seven months old. I left both my kids at home for three days and went to Mayo.

"Before I went to Mayo, Medha had called me. She was very ill and very depressed. I had heard about her illness but it was only after she came to the US that we started talking about it more often. She was very low in spirits and she was saying, 'Nothing's going to work out, it's all over.' And I said, 'Are you crazy? You have a kid to look after.' I could relate to Aryaman because of my daughter Medha.

"The three days I spent with her at Mayo were lovely. We rented a car and drove around the countryside. When Mayo said it was not going to work out, her spirits slumped again. I told her to come over to New Jersey and stay with us. She came over and was at Columbia Presbyterian."

From then on, Medha's fight was so unrelentingly feisty that Radhika who had a ringside view of it became even more of an admirer. "What attracted me to her was her positive energy, she has an amazing amount of it and I look up to her a lot," admitted Radhika unabashedly. "I have two older brothers and I found a sister in Medha. In fact, I got close to my cousin Anup because of Medha. I have learnt a lot in life from her. It's not about Anup and Medha alone. She has also done a wonderful job of bringing up Aryaman. A child who has been brought up in the lap of luxury has such great values deeply ingrained in him that the credit for it has to go to her."

Radhika vividly illustrated just what she meant by Aryaman's value-based upbringing. "He came to us one summer and spent a lot of time with us. Aryaman is a child who has never worked in the kitchen in his house but he knows life in the US. Seeing how busy I was, the way he adjusted, asking for nothing, was just so admirable. When we went shopping, there would be no splurging, no wasting money. He had a budget and he would spend within it, which is a big quality. He was not one bit enamoured by the glamour of materialistic things.

"He would help in the kitchen, make his own bed, do his laundry and pick up stuff. I went to fetch him at the airport and when I picked up his luggage, he said, 'No, *Bua*, I'll carry that myself.' We travelled from the US back to India together and he took care of me instead of it being the other way around. He was the man with me, you see," she grinned widely.

"Once, much after the transplant, Medha, Anup and all of us were at Milwaukee. We went to the mall and Aryaman wanted some chocolates. He took ten dollars from his dad and he found his chocolate for $9.99. But there was a tax on it, so he calculated it and said, 'No, I'll go for a smaller bar,' because he was short of a few pennies. That I think is a great value system.

"My husband, Mridul, is totally in love with Aryaman. He finds him highly intelligent. His curiosity and intelligence levels are very high for his age. It's all a reflection of his fine upbringing."

Radhika's admiration also stemmed from the fact that she had seen Medha critically ill, practically on the verge of slipping away, and yet living life to the fullest, even when she lay frail on a hospital bed.

The mere memory of party times at the hospital put a bright smile on Radhika's face. "For three months before the heart transplant while we waited for a donor, we had turned the hospital into a house and celebrated all festivals there. How enthusiastically Medha would participate in the hospital activities! The staff of the hospital had become family for Medha and vice-versa. For Halloween, for Christmas, they would do all the decorations in the hallways and nursing stations. Medha's biggest quality is that wherever she is at any given moment, she becomes involved with everybody there and that becomes her family. That way she is not constantly holding on to something that is not there, crying, missing and mourning. She is with the moment. She utilises every moment and makes the most of it. It was a very big move for her to leave behind her child for nearly a year.

"But she is most un-dramatic, especially for an Indian," commented Radhika. "Anup and Medha gel well because they are very similar. They know exactly what the other one wants. They found a soulmate in each other after many hits and misses. The way she takes care of Anup is so selfless. And Anup reciprocates it. It's rare to see that kind of mutual caring at this stage of life.

"What is most astonishing is that they haven't got cynical after all that they have faced. They have simply accepted the blows and treated them as a part of life. Many a time, my spirits have slumped because of the ups and downs of life and amazingly, it has been Medha who has got me out of it each time.

"I could do whatever I could for Medha because of my husband, Mridul's support. This was the only opportunity in our lives to do something for our family which is far away in India. I would have done it for anyone in the family but even more so for Medha as I always had a soft corner for her."

With a heart that's dying out on you, the interminable wait for a donor can plunge anybody into depressed patient mode. It was, however, party time when Medha lay in the hospital waiting for a heart and, "On December 8, 2001, Anup called us in the afternoon to say, the heart has come. When they heard that, my daughter Medha and Aryaman began to jump on the couch from one end to the other, shouting, 'The heart has come, the heart has come, yes, now she will get a heart.' It was as if they had got a new toy. And they wanted to go to the hospital right away. I said, 'No guys, the heart has to be fitted in.' I fixed their meal and drove alone to the hospital. It was December 8, it was raining like hell.

"I remember everything so vividly. Anup was wearing a lime green shirt with jeans. We went down to the operating room but since we were not allowed there, we decided to go to their apartment and eat something. There was no *darr*, no fear in either of us. Anup was very confident. We made *anda bhurji* (scrambled egg), had a drink each and went back to the hospital. At 3 o' clock the doctor came out and said, 'The surgery was successful, she has been shifted to the ICCU.'

"The next day we were allowed to go in and see her for a few minutes in a sanitised 'space suit'. Medha had got the heart of a 6 ft tall, 20-year-old. When the heart is freshly transplanted, it's swollen, there's oedema, so they weren't able to stitch her up. There were tons of tubes all around her body like an intricate computer network. The bed would shake with the heartbeat. Anup and I stood for a while and came back home. On the third day, Medha opened her eyes. On the fourth day, I took my daughter and Aryaman to the hospital and it was a real sight when they wore the space suit. Aryaman wasn't scared at all and the credit for that goes to Anup. He could see the confidence in his dad; he could see it all around.

"How normal all of them are! Have you noticed that despite all the negatives they have gone through, how normal a life Anup, Medha and Aryaman lead? I think Anup's motto in life is to give Medha a good time. Have fun (*maja karo, masti karo*), and don't think too much. *Sab achcha hi hoga* (all will be well).

"When I read *The Secret,* I wondered if Rhonda Byrnes had met Anup and learnt it from him. Whatever vibes you send out are what return to you. He has been practising it for years and how well it has served them.

"After her heart transplant, when Medha was discharged from the hospital on December 18, 2001, I took her to her apartment and did her *aarti* (a religious ritual). Her mother-in-law had told me to do that since she was coming home after a prolonged illness. Medha being Medha, as soon as she stepped in, she started saying, 'This thing is not in the right place, keep it there and that thing is not okay here, place it there.' I told her, '*Chhup chhaap lait jao* (keep quiet and lie down), everything is fine.' Then she went into the kitchen and wanted to make a *sabzi* (vegetable) right away. *'Mera mann kar raha hai ki ek sabzi banaoon'* (I feel like cooking). Her good friend, Tripti Mukherjee who gets panicky very quickly, started saying, 'Radhika, the heat from the cooking range will reach her heart, *lag jayegi* (she'll hurt herself).' All this was new to us. I told Tripti, 'Let her be, let's not say anything to her now.'"

Medha always maintained that without Radhika who was "the be-all and end-all for me there," the recovery would not have been possible. Radhika was dismissive of the high praise and continued, "When she was due for a transplant, 9/11 happened. There was always some significant happening other than Medha's medical condition, to keep us occupied. In 2008, when she was in a very precarious condition with fever and kidney failure, the 26/11 terror attack happened in Mumbai and that was also something all of us got very involved with. For the first time it was on CNN all the time and people were asking us, 'What's happening in Mumbai?'

"When Medha came out of the hospital after her heart transplant, the doctors had told us that she must use the washroom often. So I would keep after her and constantly ask, 'Have you gone to the bathroom? Did you do your job properly?' She got so fed up of my constant nagging that she finally turned around and threatened, 'Leave me alone or I'll stop peeing!'

"Those three months at Mount Sinai before the transplant were a breeze. We did so many fun things. One day Medha suddenly sat up and said, 'When people come to see me after the transplant, my hair won't look nice.' So we henna-ed her hair. We had *pani puri* and *bhel puri* (Indian street foods) sessions and made the nurses taste them too. It was such fun.

"But 2008 was really bad. On October 28, on Diwali day, she got hospitalised and she was discharged on December 18, 2008. That was a time when I was very scared for her. I never was earlier."

However, Medha and Anup came out of the 2008 crisis too, with enough strength to face all of 2009 on dialysis and in prepping for a kidney transplant.

"I remember when she had this fever episode for five months in 2008, and she was saying, 'Nothing is going to help me even in the US, I am not going to get all right,' she was really very dispirited. I told her, 'Leave everything, don't worry about a single thing. You don't have to even deal with the doctors, just come here.' And she did that. I had faith and my faith keeps growing stronger by the day. When she was debating where to get the kidney transplant done, I said, 'Just come here.' The kidney transplant can be done in India, that's not a major issue. It's the heart that needs to be monitored. I am so glad she is going to be under Dr Gass' care. Just the fact that he will be around will matter a lot.

"I'm sure the kidney transplant will also be a breeze. I think the worst is over. The scariest part was in 2008. I never saw Medha so low in the last eight years. I think she had just given up and accepted that the end was very close. It was the fever that had got her down so much."

Anup too, had been anxious, as Radhika disclosed, "In the hospital one day, when Medha wasn't recognising anyone and she was in severe pain, for the first time Anup hugged me and said, 'Take care of her.'"

Even as Medha hovered precariously between life and death and Anup knew just how serious it was, he had sent an SMS to a friend in Mumbai announcing, 'She's in a very bad way but I'm going to bring my wife back dancing.'

"That's his positive energy," nodded cousin Radhika. "Dr Gass also believes that the mind can work wonders. He is a doctor, scientifically and medically tuned. But he too suggests reiki, yoga, meditation for ultimate recovery."

Medha had made the same observation about Dr Gass. Every time she went for a biopsy, the procedure would be painful and unpleasant. Dr Gass would crisply say, 'I never said it's going to be a cakewalk.' Each time he did the biopsy, he would ask his patient to visualise the sky, think of the sun shining. He would use psychology and visual imagery to distract her from the pain.

It also helped that except for the rare moment when her condition made him sick with worry, Anup kept the atmosphere bright, never allowing it to get morbid.

"He was always a *mast-maula* (happy-go-lucky)," Radhika analysed. "We have learnt from him how to go through life with a healthy, positive attitude. Nothing bogs him down. Look at the setbacks he has had in life but he has always stood up and moved forward. One day, during our morning tea session when all four of us were having our *chai* (tea) together, he told us how he met and proposed to Medha. It was such a lovely story.

"I knew him when he was married to Sonali, he was his usual jolly self then too. He was very involved with his parents at that time, they were staying with him and he was working a whole lot. He did not break down when the marriage broke up.

"When you interact with Anup regularly, you realise that his conscience is very clear, very pure. I am sure his intense, devotional singing has a lot to do with his positivity and faith. He does not do pujas, he is not religious. For him religion is not about rituals or sitting in front of God but in your value system and in the good you do for others. My God, the amount of good he has done in life! He has always taken care of his family and friends and has always been a very giving person.

"Medha is also very giving," she quickly added, and followed it up with an incident to explain her remark.

"Medha came out of the hospital on December 18 and on December 22, my husband had a retinal detachment. Medha was on oxygen at home, my two children were there and Anup was in Mumbai when I took Mridul to the hospital for his retinal attachment surgery, which is a major one. And Medha was asking me, shall I come, can I help?" she recounted with a smile.

"She was on oxygen, very weak. But even at that time, Medha forgot about herself and was thinking of how we could make Mridul comfortable because he had to lie on his stomach for three weeks with no TV, no internet, no papers, no BlackBerry. She kept bothering about how we should entertain him for three weeks and forgot about her own predicament."

One could well picture the Tandon household in New Jersey with Radhika, two kids and two patients. Yet there was a singular lack of resentment that there was so much on her plate which she had to single-handedly manage.

"Wouldn't you do it for your parents or family or friends?" she countered, dismissing it as inconsequential. "It is not such a big deal. If you wish someone well, you just go out and do what you have to. I wanted Medha to regain her health. I had promised her, 'You come here; you'll heal and go back.' It became my personal battle."

The chain reaction set into motion by Anup was evident everywhere. From the rock-like bhajan singer went out such hearty positivity that it touched his wife Medha and son Aryaman. And from their firm resolve to come out of this medical imbroglio, however drastic, the positivity travelled to those around them. It was reflected in Radhika discovering an unknown power within herself.

"For me, it became a situation where I had promised her that she would be fine. How dare she not recover?" argued Radhika. "I have a lot of faith. Once, in December 2008, when I was very scared, I called up an astrologer and he said, 'It's bad, very bad.' I just hung up on him. When there is faith, nothing can stop you. Medha herself is a very determined person; if she chooses to do something, she will do it."

A point to note was the marked jubilation over every step forward, avoiding morose sombreness over the disease or its long-drawn-out treatment. It was a classic case of counting all the good that was happening and raising a toast to it without getting worked up over the many bothersome negatives.

In the midst of all her compelling problems, Medha would size up those around her and pull them up if they dared look unhealthy.

"Medha likes fit people. If I lose 10 kilos, she will love me a little more," laughed Radhika. Ironically, "Medha is someone who has always looked after herself."

Radhika also drew attention to the fact that the presence of so many different people around her was indicative of the kind of person Medha herself was.

One of the many friends that Radhika talked about was Odissi dancer Daksha Mashruwala who was Medha's neighbour in Beach House, Juhu, when she was still married to Shekhar Kapur. It was her fondness for the fine arts that brought Medha close to Daksha.

Essentially a Bharat Natyam dancer who moved to Odissi, Daksha and Medha were both learning Hindustani classical music from the same teacher, Pandit Jasraj's disciple, Mukesh Desai. It was Mukesh who mentioned to Daksha that he was also teaching Shekhar Kapur's wife, Medha, who lived in the same building.

"My first introduction to Medha was through classical music," noted Daksha. It was an introduction Daksha was reluctant to make. "I wasn't so sure about meeting a celebrity wife," she sheepishly recalled. "But Medha simply came down one day and we clicked instantly. She had just come from Delhi and was doing up her house. Once we met, I couldn't believe that she was such a down-to-earth person. Since then, we have got along really well. It has been like a journey together.

"I was trying to find a dance institution for myself in Mumbai and I finally found Kelucharan Mohapatra. Medha was so interested in dance that she came with me everywhere, and everybody thought she was also a dancer because she has that look about her. She has always been there at all our programmes and workshops. For my first solo Odissi stage programme, she had vacated her living room, kept a tape recorder and said, 'Come and practice here.' It was that kind of friendship. We shared everything, dance, music, we even went shopping together."

Such a close friendship with Medha also meant that Daksha was privy to all her ups and downs over the years. "She was in Beach House for a few years. I was very much around when her split with Shekhar Kapur happened," stated Daksha. "I have only one daughter who was very young then. So I was a little home-bound those days. With Medha so close by, it was breakfast at her place or Gujju lunch at mine."

Watching Medha go through a buffet of experiences, Daksha came to some firm conclusions about her friend's character. "When the Shekhar Kapur split happened, it was very gradual, not a sudden occurrence," explained Daksha. "The most striking quality that I have consistently found in Medha is her truthfulness. Even in her relationship with Shekhar, everything was extremely honest. She is what she is. I think that's why she gets along with so many different people. She doesn't have one group. My husband and I have a lifestyle that is different from hers. So on anniversaries, birthdays and functions, when she would throw a party, we wondered if we would fit in. But having been close to her right since her Shekhar days, then Vinod, then Anup, we got to know her various friends. I still remember the whole discussion when Anup proposed to her – it was so superb talking it over together.

"Being with Medha has been like watching life through a friend and learning lessons from it. I learnt from her how to take everything in my stride with a smile. I had a standard homely life with my in-laws. But with her I got to see several lifetimes in one.

"One could see the Shekhar split coming. She was home-loving and she was lonely. It was a great friendship with Shekhar but she wanted the joy of having a home and a family.

"Initially, I wasn't sure about Anup, I didn't know much about him. But there were times when Medha and I would make fun of Anup's singing because we were such hardcore classical music lovers. People told me that I had to warn Medha about Anup's reputation. I did pass that on to her but she felt so loved and wanted that she wanted to be with him. That was the phase when she was feeling a very strong rejection from Vinod. It was a natural desire to want love and to respond to it.

"Medha is very real and she doesn't portray herself as someone different. She is the same whether she is with me, with my daughter, my father-in-law or my dog, or my maids. My maids adore her and it's not because she is a celebrity. Till today, when she comes home, she will have at least one sentence to share with everyone in the house. She is a complete people's person. What attracts me to her is her multi-dimensional personality. Medha has so many interests in life. She constantly wants to live life fully.

"Her life-threatening diseases are an irony. It's the biggest mystery that someone who is so full of life has been on the brink of losing it so often. Sometimes when she's feeling slightly low, I tell her that she is this one big example we cite to everybody. All that's happening to Medha is too amazing. We can't get over the fact that it's not stopping, things keep happening and happening to her and she's taking it all.

"I don't know where that strength comes from. Sometimes I think it's Aryaman who's giving her so much strength. Then I realise that she's not even a typical clingy type of mother. I think she just knows how to live every moment.

"She hardly talks of her ailments and complaints. Sometimes I have to probe and ask, what's happening next? But that has never been the focus of her conversation. When she had a kidney transplant around the corner, she was here to check out what renovations we had done in the kitchen!

"When we went shopping, she would go, 'No, not this tumbler, with this bucket, take this one.' Every little thing had to be matched and presented well. Nobody would believe that she was so enthusiastic about such sundry things when she was actually on dialysis and waiting for a kidney donor.

My father-in-law, who's 87 and has seen her all these years, wonders at Medha. He and everybody else just want to smile and welcome her because she is so pleasant even in this state. She is a very rare and fascinating personality, the perfect subject for a book.

"Medha is the sort of person who attracts a variety of people to her. Look at the kind of people who have come into her life. And look at Anupji. As fascinated as I am about how Medha is taking her illness, I'm equally fascinated with him.

"Before the transplant, when she was at Lilavati Hospital, Mumbai, and water was filling up in her stomach, I was busy with classes during the day, so it was understood that the night shift would be mine. I used to actually look forward to that because we could spend time together. It was such fun. And to think we are talking about a very ill person in the hospital!

"She is always very proper, the way she dresses, the way she behaves. One afternoon at the hospital in Mumbai, her stomach had bloated quite a bit. Every month they had to do tapping which meant two-three days in the hospital. The nurse said that the doctor was on his way. Medha quickly asked for her bag, took out her lipstick, her blush, her eye pencil, she did her hair, made herself up, completely covered her stomach with a blanket and sat up. She didn't want to look like a patient. She did herself up so naturally, she looked lovely and charming. Who would have thought of doing that in her condition?

"In New York, during those three weeks before her transplant, her mother was also there. Medha was in the hospital and hadn't even seen the apartment she was moving into but she got it completely furnished to her taste. From the curtains to the cushions, mats, napkins, her mom and I would go shopping and buy them. Medha would look up catalogues and decide what she wanted and without having seen that flat even once, she did it up exactly as she wanted it to be.

"Medha was so picky about things, sometimes she would reject what we had bought saying, 'This is not nice, that will go better with it.' Our time would just fly by with all that. Her mom would suddenly remember that there was a sale in some shop and off we would go.

"While waiting for the heart, she had tubes all over her. Before I left for New York, Eeda had prepared me for what I would see but even then, when I saw Medha, I couldn't control my tears. She had become like a skeleton. But even in that condition, she was doing some crochet or doing up her apartment by remote control from her hospital bed."

It came naturally to Medha to immerse herself in sundry pursuits, leaving no room for darkness to enter her being. Her lively disposition also helped turn the long stay in the hospital into a pleasant social do where other patients became the friendly neighbours next door.

She had managed to do that even when she was hospitalised in Mumbai. Talat Aziz recalled that Medha and Anup had once requested him to be the Chief Guest at a function in Hinduja Hospital where she herself was a patient.

"In the nephrology wing, there was a gathering of people who had gone through a kidney transplant," narrated Talat. Anup couldn't attend the function since he had to go elsewhere for a concert.

"All the patients with their relatives were there and Medha was sitting right in front. She was a patient but she had taken the trouble to organise something for a function there!

"They wanted me to sing something which I did, then I sat next to her. There was a young patient in her 20s whose teenage brother had donated his kidney to her. She was recounting her story, there were others from different villages. Medha sat through all that and only when she was tired did she ask for her wheelchair to go back to her room."

Talat's Mumbai hospital story found an echo in Daksha's observations of Medha in New York during her long wait for a heart donor. She had turned the hospital ward into her temporary abode, delighting in living in the moment.

"Her social interaction with the others in the hospital was wonderful," Daksha described the pre-transplant days in New York. "There were two other patients, besides Medha, who were also waiting for a heart. There was a young Spanish guy and a slightly elderly Jewish man called Joseph. In the evening we would join them and play cards, we would joke about various things, it was such a good atmosphere. Medha and I would walk around the ward with her stand that had tubes all over. The vibrations that Medha sent out all around the hospital were incredible. She did all this while she was facing a grave illness and hadn't met her son for nearly a year.

"Those were incredible times. I used to wear typical Indian salwar-kameezes with a big bindi on my forehead. Very amused by it, Joseph wanted to know about 'that red circle you wear on your forehead.' We explained everything about the bindi to him. One day Joseph came to Medha's room with a red thing on his forehead. Because he was Jewish, his plate of food had a red mark to indicate a special meal. He took that mark, wore it like a bindi and came to show it to us. It was hilarious."

Hearing Daksha narrate the fun times took the edge off the anxiety and worry that must have dogged Medha somewhere in the subterranean layers of her system. It stayed there and wasn't ever allowed to surface.

Daksha recalled, "I think it was their Thanksgiving or some such occasion and Medha's mother had gone out and got little gifts for everybody. She got some teddy bears with hearts for Medha and she got Joseph also a gift with a heart sticker. After about two-three hours, Joseph came to the door with the heart sticker on his hospital shirt. From the door he told Medha, 'I have a new heart.' Medha thought he was referring to the stickers, so she replied, 'Even I have two hearts.' She had hung her hearts on the pole. I get goose flesh when I talk about this but Joseph didn't have the courage to tell Medha that just before he came to our room, he had got a call that he had actually got a donor; he had really got a new heart. When Medha realised what he was saying, her eyes filled up, she was so happy for him; all of us were. By late evening, he went in for the transplant but he never came out alive."

Those were the realities that surrounded a hospital bed and keeping the amiability alive was a test of mental strength. It was a whole new culture, the intimate hospital way of life that Daksha witnessed with Medha in the centre of it and contributing to maintain the warmth, even as the cold facts of life, disease and death, constantly hovered around them.

"When Joseph had come to our door," Daksha continued, "while he was joyous at having got a donor, he was simultaneously feeling bad to tell Medha. She was younger than him and he knew that she had also been waiting for long for a heart. But Medha was genuinely very happy for him.

"Joseph used to be alone in his room and that day, he couldn't share his news with anyone from his family. He couldn't get in touch with his wife or his family in Israel. So Medha gave him her mobile to call Israel and talk to his people. He broke the news to his family from Medha's mobile.

"Her mother and I both left before Medha got her heart. It was all so much like a fairy tale. How much her mother prayed! Every morning she would put on the *'Maha Mritunjay'* tape and pray that the donor comes when she was still there. She wanted to be there with Medha during the transplant. But she had a fall and the girls decided that she should go back to India. Soon Anup surprised Medha with Aryaman's visit and she got a heart immediately after he arrived. I can't believe that such things actually happen."

Daksha was equally wonderstruck at Medha's miraculous recovery, not once but four times when medical science had given up on her. She said, astonished, "I wonder what keeps Medha so charged, so alive through all those setbacks. Like I said earlier, is it Aryaman? But she's not a typical mother. She just loves life so much, she radiates life, and she is not giving up. It also has something to do with the tremendous support she has, of course from her family but from Anup and Aryaman too. He is such a small kid and she keeps going off for dialysis every other day.

"For the first four-and-a-half years after the transplant, life was really beautiful for them. Then the kidney failure started, Medha would have fever and discomfort. So many times I would be with her in her room when Aryaman would come back from school. He knew exactly what was happening but he was never under any tension. He is not a traumatised child. How can a child be so strong? Mother, sisters, husband, one can understand that they are all grown-ups. But a little child? He could be like that only if Medha didn't dramatise her complaints. She never played the patient even when she was in severe pain, especially in her legs. There was one little pleasure she would get and that was in getting her legs massaged. More like a joke she would say, now that you have come, *zara zor se daba de* (press them harder). Everything was with that fabulous sense of humour.

"Another trait of hers in the hospital was that she was always so aware and so particular about her medicines. She would be meticulous about taking her medicines. She would read her file and if there was any little change, she would catch the nurse. A complete perfectionist, she has to keep her house, her medicines, her files, everything in order.

"Before the transplant, there was a tube, 24×7 in her neck. Every few days, they would change it from the left side to the right. It was painful for her but she was so practical about it. She would say, 'Oh, tomorrow I have to go there to change the tube, I better shampoo my hair.' She was that particular, everything had to be clean and proper. Even now, the way she plans her days is so meticulous. On non-dialysis days what she's going to do, that diary of hers is so up-to-date. Sometimes I feel maybe she values her life and doesn't want to waste even a day. But she doesn't talk or philosophise about it that way.

"There is a particular sincerity in everything she does. Once, we tried *pranic* healing (faith-healing) while at Lilavati. We would laugh at it but she did try it out in good faith. She tried feng shui, gemmology, everything in right earnest. But at the same time she wouldn't go at it fanatically. Ultimately, she had utmost faith only in herself."

But Medha was only human and there were the occasional dips in her moods. At such times, close friend Bina Aziz was someone Medha could turn to. "One day we were going for a drive," said Bina, "and Medha was saying, 'How can I constantly talk about my illness to everybody? But I do get depressed, I wonder, why does this keep happening?' And I told her, 'As friends we understand, it's not easy to go through what you have undergone. Anything you want to talk about, just feel free to talk to us any time.' That's the least we can do as friends. It's so important to let it out.

"A couple of months ago, she was feeling a little low and just wanted to go out of her house, take her mind off her illness for some time. I told her to come over to my place and arranged a nice massage for her at the parlour. I thought a good reflexology, foot massage would be the best relaxation for her. We went there, she had her massage and went back. It took her mind off her problems for that moment and she felt good."

Fortunately, Medha rarely hit a low or gave up on life. "She hasn't really given up except for very short periods," commented Daksha. "Like the time she ran away from Lilavati. I had been there at night and in the morning when Anupji was there she had run away. She called me up and joked, *'Main bhaagke aa gayi'* (I've run away). It was a joke because by then she had got control over herself. But she had run away out of total frustration. I asked her if she wasn't afraid but she said it was only when she was crossing the road and hailing a taxi that she felt a little frightened. 'But I couldn't take it anymore,' she said. And then it became funny because she had left Anup back there in hospital, totally befuddled."

Along with the humour were also the nightmarish days when the pain would make Medha cry out and move those around her. There was one particularly heart-wrenching day after her kidneys failed.

"Once at Hinduja Hospital, there have been so many procedures done on her, I don't remember all the names but everything had failed," shuddered Daksha. "We were all taking turns being with her. I reached the hospital and was on her floor but before I could reach her room, there was this awful screaming. I could feel it was Medha's voice but it was impossible, she had never screamed like that. I got frightened as they had closed the curtain and were doing something to her. Sunita Prem Kishen was there, no one else. The nurses were all bustling around and I was frightened because that scream in her semi-conscious state was something I had never heard. I had never seen her in that much pain even in her pre-transplant days when her heart had failed. Anup had left that morning for a programme, so we called up Eeda. She came in the afternoon and she also broke down. It was a very dark period when her kidneys were really in a bad condition."

That was Medha in a near-coma. But once she was out of it, she dared to go out and party within a fortnight, chuckled Daksha.

"Soon after that, she had her birthday at Golden Orchid and every single person she called was there. People were shocked because she was so very frail. She walked in late but she looked so beautiful that day. It was a pleasant surprise because just two weeks ago we were not sure if she would live.

"At the hospital when she had screamed, Sunita was telling her GP, 'You cannot say that we're trying, that's not good enough, you have to get her out of it.'

"And two weeks later, Medha had her birthday party! Medha has perfected the art of camouflaging whichever part of the body has a big mark or something. She is so particular about not flaunting her illness, not making it obvious. There have been no hysterics, no histrionics. At the most she will call me and say, *'Aa jaana na'* (please drop by). And you can tell that she's a little down, she needs to be cheered up.

"Right through her illnesses, we were all part of a patchwork who had come together to be with Medha. All her friends, Sunita, Tani, none of us were connected. But suddenly we were taking each other's numbers down because we were taking turns to be with Medha."

What comes through clearly is that all through Medha's and Anup's over-11-year ordeal, an astounding array of family members and friends stood vigil over the patient round-the-clock, never once withdrawing their support.

The question was: why would a childhood friend like Tani (Delhi) or Daksha (Mumbai) spring a ticket to New York to look after an ailing Medha? Why would family and friends like Radhika Tandon, Madhu, Tripti or Ashok Bajaj who lead a hectic, do-it-all-yourself lifestyle in the US, make so much time for a gravely ill patient? What was it about Medha and Anup that such a cross-section of people were drawn towards them? Why did they all pitch in and help so generously with their time and hospitality?

Answers emanated from New York-based textile industrialist Ashok Bajaj who put his unique equation with Medha and Anup into sharp perspective.

"My wife Gargi has been close to Anup right from childhood and over the years I also developed a warm friendship with him," said Ashok Bajaj before adding, "I cannot give a name to our equation. I can't say, my friend, my brother. Let's just call it a human-to-human relationship.

"I met Medha for the first time when they had come to New York and were staying at the Lexington, a Taj hotel. She struck me as a nice, friendly person and I was happy that Anup had met her. As I got to know Medha better, I found her an intelligent, fun-loving person.

"When she came to the US with arrhythmia for the first time, we never looked at it as something very serious. In fact, Gargi and I went to Mayo to be with her for about three days and we thought it would only be an investigation and she would be fine. I had heard about arrhythmia and I never thought it would be such a complicated disease.

"But when they accidentally ruptured one of her arteries, it was a major shock for us. Though rare, mishaps do happen sometimes. The unfortunate part was that it happened to us. Doctors always warn a patient that once they go in, anything could happen. That's why there is a big fear of surgery. But you get attracted by the numbers. They have done thousands of similar surgeries and 97 per cent are successful. Nobody claims 100 per cent success. But you always feel, 'I will be one of the 97 per cent,' you never think you could be a part of the unsuccessful 2 or 3 per cent.

"However, the anger lasted only for a short time because the strength to move on came to us from Anup and Medha themselves. They are such positive people, I was stunned at the way they handled every situation. We have never ever seen either of them go, '*Haai, main bimar ho gayi, haai main mar gayi, haai, ye kya ho gaya, main kya karoongi, mere husband ka kya hoga, mere bachche ka kya hoga?*' (I'm so ill, I'm going to die, how did this happen, what'll I do, what'll happen to my husband, my child?) Never have we heard them wail or complain. In fact, they are our motivation for positivity and strength.

"Only once, sometime in 2008-9, Medha called me from Mumbai and said, 'Ashok Bhai, *main thak gayi*' (I'm tired of it all) and I said, 'This is the first time you've said it and I never want to hear you utter these words again. *Aap nahin thak sakte ho, kisi haal mein bhi* (you cannot get tired, come what may), you can't talk like that. You cannot give up, you cannot get negative. It's your positivity that has taken you so far, you cannot tire of it. I don't want to hear this again from you.' She called me the next day and said, 'Ashokbhai, you were right. I'm not going to talk like that.' Anup has also remained positive all through. Even if we ever talked of the mounting expenses, he would say, 'Don't worry, *ho jayega*' (it'll get sorted out). It became a favourite phrase of his to say, *'Ho jayega'* all the time. Be it in his profession, or in the handling of a social or family problem, I have never seen this guy angry or in a negative mode. Even in business, when things have gone against him, Anup would say, 'Ashok, it's fine, don't worry, it's okay.' I used to ask him at such times, 'Are you human or some kind of God to be like this?' He would laugh and tell me, 'You sing bhajans, you will also become like this,' and I would repartee, 'In my next life, I will sing bhajans with you.'

"I absolutely believe that it is his bhajan singing, his devotional, meditative singing that has given him the strength and the positive attitude to face so many setbacks with such calm. I wouldn't like to call it superhuman strength because I believe that this is how humans should be."

Ashok Bajaj was privileged to witness the uplifting effect of Anup's full-throated singing on the listener, many times over. It happened once at the Prime Minister's residence in New Delhi when Atal Bihari Vajpayee invited Anup and all his close circle of friends to his house for Ram Navmi (Lord Rama's birthday).

"Atalji had a very select gathering of VIPs that day. Every one of his 50 to 60 invitees was a valued guest. Vyjayanthimala, Manmohan Singh, a few top ministers were all there. For about one-and-a-half to two hours, Anup sang all the bhajans relevant to Ram Navmi. Believe me, right through his concert, Vyjayanthimala was crying. Anup has that ability to reach deep inside and touch the heart. I have heard him so many times, gone to so many of his concerts. Even at home, he sits around singing. But every time he sings a bhajan, he manages to sound different and stir you emotionally. He is simply mesmerising. You can hear the same bhajan from him 110 times and each time he will evoke a different feeling in you. That's the magic of his music.

"Atalji got up and wanted to honour him but Anup requested him to wait. He came down from the stage and went up to meet the Prime Minister. Everybody had tears in their eyes that day. His singing was so moving, it was unbelievable. His bhajans have definitely given Anup a lot of power to make him what a real human being should be."

Medha and Anup always maintained that the staunch support provided by Ashok helped them face their traumatic experiences in New York. "No, no," reacted Ashok instantly. "That is their *badappan* (greatness). I haven't really done anything. It is only God's hand. He shows the path to all of us. *Eeshwar sab karvata hai*, we are the puppets He uses. *Main yogya nahin hoon* to do anything. It's not me, it is destiny, God's will. He makes the plans and He executes them. I am honoured if Medha and Anup feel this way about me but it was their own karma that came to their aid.

"I'm a semi-retired person. My work doesn't need me every second. It's not a nine-to-five job, so I could take out some time to be with them when they needed it. There was support from everybody in my family. You need the wholehearted support, adjustment and understanding of the entire family to do anything in life. But whatever we could do for them came to us naturally."

Refreshingly, Ashok Bajaj also revealed a dimension to Anup that had largely remained unknown. If people rallied around Medha and Anup, the celebrity-singer also found the time to be present on every important occasion in the Bajaj family.

"They build relationships, they are like magnets. They attract people, you get pulled towards them. And they attract you in times of celebration also," pointed out Ashok.

"When my son, Kunal, got married in 2001, we came down from the US to have the marriage in India. Right from the beginning, Anup used to say that whenever Kunal got married, he would take care of his function in India. When the time came, Medha was in New York, waiting for a donor for her heart transplant. Anup kept assuring me that he would be with us but I knew that they had problems of their own. So I contacted some other musicians, paid them an advance and made my own arrangements for a function in Delhi. Four-five days before the cocktail party, Anup called and said, 'I'm in India for a concert, I will be reaching your function and I will be with all of you.' I told him that I had already made my arrangements and that he needed to be with Medha. He said, 'No, I had promised you,' and he turned up with all his musicians. I went to the people I had earlier arranged and paid them some more money saying, 'Sorry but Anupji is coming to sing.' The stage was ready, everything was set when Anup suddenly asked me for a car because Medha had got a donor and he had to rush to New York. We arranged the car and believe me, I didn't think even for one minute of all the arrangements that I had already cancelled. Now I had nobody to entertain the guests, we were having this big cocktail party and looking forward to a big celebration. His musicians said, 'We'll manage,' but I didn't know what to do. Anyway, we got involved with some ceremonial puja, and when we came out, we found Anup standing there. He said, 'It was a false alarm, the donor didn't match, so I have come back to sing at your function.' Medha had called him up and said, 'You go to Kunal's function first and then come to New York.'

"That's the kind of people they are. They are a part of your body. They are there for us too, all the time.

"When they came back from the US empty-handed after the kidney donor was rejected in 2010, it must have been a major jolt for them. Anybody else would have given up. But the kind of will power Medha has is unbelievable. There is no comparison, it is peerless. She's a fighter and that is what keeps her alive."

The following story gave evidence of the warmth that Anup invested in a relationship. Ashok narrated, "Anup was in New York and staying with me. I had some cousins and my *Maasi* (maternal aunt) also visiting from India. My aunt had an accident and she could not attend his concert while everybody else went to hear him. The next morning, while the rest of us were having our tea, Anup quietly went to my aunt's room and for a full hour he sat by her feet and sang his bhajans. He said to her, 'Yesterday you couldn't come and hear me, so today I have come here to sing for you.' What a wonderful gesture! I can give you so many instances of his graceful nature.

"Another time, almost 25 years ago, I had gone to Delhi on some work and Anup had come there to Talkatora for a concert. All my partners and friends told me that they had got tickets to hear him sing and asked me to come along. I said, 'No, don't ask me because I am really too tired to stir out, I want to sleep.' Anup had no clue that I was also in Delhi. The concert had already started when I decided to go and join them. It was a packed hall. When the door opened and Anup saw me, he said in mid-concert, 'Ashokji, *aap kahan se aa gaye?*' (where have you come from?) And from the stage he instructed someone to put a chair in front for me to sit. With everybody watching, Anupji stopped his concert midway to talk to me and I felt so self-conscious. But that's the kind of man he is.

"Medha is also like that," added Ashok Bajaj. "At the hospital I used to tell the doctors and others that I was her brother-in-law. But she used to say, he is not my brother-in-law, he is my angel-in-law. I used to stop her from saying that because I felt, '*Yeh sab Prabhu ki ichcha hoti hai*' (it is God's will).

"We always hope that she comes out of her problems. She has the will power but she is still suffering, she is experiencing pain on a daily basis and we cannot do anything about it. That hurts us. We cannot take away her pain. Unfortunately, she has to go through it."

Gargi and Ashok Bajaj go back a long way with Anup which could explain why they put themselves out on a limb to help the beleaguered couple. But why did a public school teacher, a New Yorker called Madhu Seth who met Medha only after she had fallen ill, give the patient so much tender loving care?

Medha's Nirmal *Maasi* had contacted Madhu, her family friend in New York, and told her that her niece who was critically ill, was coming into New York for treatment. So, would Madhu please keep an eye on her? That was Madhu's first contact with Medha, "A person for whom I have the greatest admiration."

A couple of weeks after Nirmal *Maasi*'s call, Madhu heard from Anup's cousin, Radhika Tandon. "Radhika told me that Medha had been admitted to Mount Sinai," said Madhu, recollecting her first meeting with Medha. "I went to meet her after school. Medha was sitting up cheerfully on her hospital bed with a bloated belly, looking rather pregnant. The image of 'very ill' did not fit the lady in bed. I introduced myself and she greeted me warmly with a very infectious smile. Anupji was on the phone. She explained very calmly to me that water had to be drained out of her abdomen and that she had to undergo a major surgery for her heart which was weakening every day. I could not believe that this figure of serenity was so cool and relaxed about her physical state. Nothing in her voice was seeking sympathy. On the contrary, she was bright and supremely optimistic. That's what struck me about Medha at our first meeting.

"In the next few weeks, I got to know Medha and Anupji better and even though I was very concerned, her optimism enveloped me. I read up articles on the high success of modern heart transplant operations and also collected stories of post-transplant acts of great physical and mental courage.

"I would often go over to meet her after my school but when I hadn't heard from her for about a week, I decided to pay her an unexpected visit at the hospital. I got the shock of my life when I came to know that she had been operated two days earlier and was in intensive care. I was annoyed at myself for not having inquired after her mid-week. I always wanted to be there for her. All these thoughts raced through my mind when I approached Bed No 2. To my utter horror, this was a Medha I had never pictured. She was all shrivelled up, dark, wrinkly, thin, with what looked like a hundred tubes running in and out of her.

I stammered, 'Medha, how are you doing?' She rolled her sleepy, drugged eyes, managed a bit of a smile and said, 'Now I am fine. How are you?' In that condition, she was enquiring about my health! I managed to say, 'Fine.' I asked her why she was sitting up so soon after her operation and she informed me, 'I have been told to do so for an hour or two. I have been given morphine to numb the pain. Can you tell me the oxygen level? It is on the top right side of the monitor.' I read out the level to her. She asked me to check the heartbeat rate. What stayed with me was how much control she had over her mind and body even at a time like that. What an amazing patient! She even told me to ask my son Uday not to smoke and added that he should see her in her present state to understand that this could happen to him too. I tried to change the topic and asked her what the doctors had to say. She answered, 'Dr Gass said I will be fine in some time. But an astrologer has told me that this is a very crucial time in my life. If I live through this day, I will live for a long time.' 'You are going to do very well,' I replied. Her contagious optimism had infected us through and through. I left wondering how this shrivelled-up figure would survive. It was hard to control myself and I had to go to the restroom to drain out my fears and tears. She was in so much pain and not talking about it, optimistically looking to enjoy the sunrise. And here I was, bringing the roof down over the threading of my eyebrow. I vowed, 'Never again will I scream when in pain.'"

The shrivelled-up figure made such a startling recovery that it left everybody agape with wonder.

"Hours turned to days, days into weeks and weeks into months. The colour was coming back into her cheeks, the sparkle back into her eyes (it never did leave her); her skin was getting back its original glow. The optimism never dulled or eclipsed even for a moment. She was constantly monitoring and controlling what was good for her.

"Medha had moved into her apartment on Upper East Side. We met up occasionally. I would stop by after school. On one such occasion, Anupji was visiting. It was her birthday. She was very happy and there was a gleam in her eye when she said that Anupji had written a sweet little poem for her. I implored him to read it out to me. He did that with joy, every word idolising her and his love for her. His words seem to bring her to life. There was so much devotion and love that as usual, I went back completely influenced and showered my husband with love and affection.

"On July 4, the US celebrates its Independence and it gives us a reason to party. We invited a few close friends to watch the fireworks from our window. After the fireworks, the viewing party became a dance party and Medha was at her graceful best till late at night. Another side to her was that she would not let her ill health or weakened condition take over her life.

"Winter, spring, summer and then comes autumn. Almost a year was complete. It was Karva Chauth (a day when north Indian women fast for their husbands) and I asked Medha if she would like to come over and join the puja at my place. Not only did she come, she dutifully kept the fast too. A year wasn't yet complete after her heart transplant. By Jove, that was some devotion!"

Medha never played the convalescent which probably helped her go through critical periods like an unaffected, healthy person would. As Madhu observed, "All through the seasons, I have only seen her cheerful, careful about her health and in total control of herself. To top it, always looking glamorous. For several years,

Medha and Anupji kept coming to New York for her checkup, at least twice a year. We would meet up and her demeanour would always be optimistic, hopeful and looking up to the sun."

The one time Medha seemed to lose control and go into a dark cloud was in late 2008 when an inexplicable fever struck and she hovered between life and death.

"Her sudden arrival shook us," said Madhu. "She had been running fever and was admitted to the hospital. For the first time, I felt her morale going under. She was heavily sedated but managed to open her eyes and say, 'Madhu, I'm very ill.' My heart sank and I could only see clouds of dismay mist my eyes. I had never known her to give up. Reassuring her that she would come out of this too, I finished my shift to watch over her and howled all the way home." The fantastic highlight was that Medha managed to pull out of it that time too.

Madhu remembered that when it was her turn to sleep at the hospital, Medha was unfailingly considerate, however critical her own condition. "Medha would ensure that I had eaten, that I was comfortable and that I slept well."

It was a recurring observation by almost all her care-givers that Medha was grateful and aware of the people rallying around her. To all of them, she showed a caring side of her personality, most times suppressing her own discomfort.

If friends and family drew strength, hope and positivity from a gravely ill patient (instead of it being the other way around), Dr Jatin Kothari at Hinduja Hospital, Mumbai, saw in Medha a unique patient, one he had rarely encountered in his illustrious career.

At the young age of 40, nephrologist Dr Kothari had risen to the top of his profession and had treated a wide spectrum of ill people but none to beat this celebrity-patient. But first a quick glance at Medha's medical report as recorded by this specialist:

"My first interaction with Medha was in 2007 when she was consulting a team of physicians in our hospital. Dr Kapadia, an intensive care specialist and general physician, was treating Medha for some of her post-heart transplant issues. The doctors found that she had a kidney problem which was probably due to the immune-suppressive medication she was on after the transplant. Some of those medicines are known to cause problems with the kidney functions. So that's how I came into the picture.

"In the first six months, her condition worsened quite rapidly and she has been on dialysis ever since. As we talk, we're looking forward to a kidney transplant and that's going to be one more major change for her."

Dr Kothari remembered an occasion when Medha almost didn't survive a serious complication. "Along with the heart issues, Medha had a problem of fluid accumulation in the abdomen," he explained. "She would get an infection in that fluid which would make her very sick. You had to give her a course of antibiotics for it. But after the kidney problem surfaced, she was once admitted in the ICU here because of a serious stomach infection and that was one time she almost did not make it. She was in the hospital for nearly a month, including two weeks in the ICU. She was very, very sick at that time."

This was in 2007-2008 and Dr Kothari witnessed first-hand one of Medha's miraculous recoveries because he was one of the many who had thought that it would be curtains for her this time around.

"Amazingly, when things turn around in her case, there are factors which we cannot explain by science alone," he accepted. "Throughout her ICU stint and illness, when she was in the hospital for a very long period, Medha and her husband remained remarkably positive. She pulled through when some of us in the team doubted if she would make it. Yes, I was one of them," he admitted frankly. "By that time dialysis had started, so most of the time she was pretty much under my care and our primary focus was to try and get her out of the kidney issue.

"The teamwork was exceptionally good and because of the Jalotas' unwavering positivity, she was able to get through all the difficult phases. Then she went to the US again to get an evaluation of her heart, to check how well the heart was faring and touch wood, everything was cleared on that front. The doctors told her that there was no rejection of the heart. So everything was back on track. She took about six months to recover from the problems she had during her stay and gradually she built up well in terms of nutrition and health."

Whenever Dr Kothari was a bit hazy with the dates in his narrative, he would stop and recommend that the details be procured from Medha herself because she was just so meticulous with her medical records. "She gets all her files updated and all her reports are neatly filed date-wise. At any point, she can tell you exactly what happened and when. She's very particular about getting things right and keeping track of everything.

"She is a rare, unbelievable patient. We don't really come across patients who do such excellent follow-up. Despite her having so many major medical problems, she almost never disturbs us in terms of our routine work. If there is something urgent that needs to be addressed, she will send an absolutely pertinent text message with specific questions that need to be answered. I also prefer it that way because sometimes it is very difficult to communicate serious issues like the ones she has, over the phone.

So she is the kind of patient that you would love to have although you don't want anyone to suffer from kidney failure."

An astute aside could be made here that Medha was meticulous about her treatment because she didn't really have a choice. Or, was it because she really was a very different kind of patient?

"It's probably a combination of both," Dr Kothari analysed. "She has very limited options for sure because she is probably one of the very few patients in this country who has had a heart transplant and is now going in for another major organ transplant. This is not common in this part of the world and given her social circumstances, to face her problem so painstakingly makes her unique in a lot of ways.

"Science also has its limitations and we can't offer her just about every treatment that we offer other patients. She is different because she also probably does not have a lot of choices. She has gone through a lot of doctors and hospitals across the world, so she knows how she has to be taken care of and how her medical issues have to be sorted out. All this makes her a different kind of patient for us. It is interesting to discuss her medical issues with her because her acumen in understanding her disease is very high. She understands her disease more than any one of us, that's for sure," remarked the nephrologist. "That's why her questions are very specific. She knows which questions to ask me, what has to be addressed to a particular person. If it is related to the heart, she'll drop an email to her cardiologist in the US and get her answers from there. This way she has done remarkably well.

"It has been a very good interaction with Medha," he went on. "She is really such a unique patient that even in the dialysis unit, she leaves us amazed. Most of the time her blood pressure is very low and it's something that most of us taking care of her are very worried about. But she is still so positive about it. She knows what has to be done with the dialysis prescription and she motivates the other patients to also come for regular dialysis. Most of them don't know her story in detail but they get a lot of confidence from knowing that a person with a heart transplant can so cheerfully do dialysis eight years down the line before eventually going in for a kidney transplant. That's really good for us because she motivates other patients and it works well for them.

"In my career here in India, she is the first heart-transplant patient who is under my care. I did manage a few multi-organ transplant patients when I was training in Canada but no one in our country. Here, we have treated a few liver transplant patients who have developed some mild kidney problems but no one who has had a major organ transplant and has come to us for dialysis.

"Most patients in her condition would be down and out but that's not something she ever thinks about. She's always looking at what the next step should be and looks forward to other channels. She is an emotional person too, but she's able to control herself well. At times, we have all wondered how she is able to keep up with these major issues where there are not many things to look forward to. There have been times when we would get depressed while going through her case history and do a recap of all that she has gone through in the last few years. But these are matters that she never points out. That's probably her strength, that's perhaps why she has been able to pull on for so long."

Dr Kothari was experienced enough to acknowledge that sometimes exemplary courage cropped up in times of crisis and Medha was perhaps a good example of this syndrome. As he remarked, "Most patients who go through a chronic medical illness like hers do find the courage from somewhere to face it. We see this in patients who have cancer and kidney disease that are chronic in nature. It's an ongoing battle for them, especially for patients who have transplants because they need to go through a major change in their lifestyle for the rest of their lives. These patients get stronger as they go along. Those that don't do well, we don't hear about because they don't survive.

But," he pointed out, "in Medha's case, it is an extremely unique strength that we have witnessed. We would have never thought that hers would be such a case especially because of the social circumstances that she is in. Finance is, by God's grace, not a problem for her. Otherwise, most patients in our country struggle through the financial burden of such chronic treatment. But she also has a remarkably strong will to live. She has her agendas, she has her agenda for the next week and the next month and she looks forward to life. That's also probably what keeps her going.

"It has not been proven medically but it is a well-known fact and it has been published in medical journals too, that patients who have a positive outlook towards their disease do much better than those who do not have it. So it is a psychosomatic approach to chronic medical problems which has kept her going.

"I have never seen her give up. Not even when she was seriously ill and some of us had lost hopes of her ever recovering. We thought it would be very difficult for her and that she would opt for not taking dialysis at all because, in between, when the heart was not doing very well, even the kidney transplant equation was looking very difficult. It was all very complicated because the doctors mentioned that they wanted the heart to settle down before they put her up for a kidney transplant. We thought she would break down when all this came up but she faced it and has done amazingly well." Dr Kothari was also extremely aware that being an ideal patient was tough on a critically ill person but Medha came up trumps on more than one occasion.

"She tries to follow whatever advice is given to her. At times, it is very easy for us to dispense advice and say, follow this diet and take these medicines but I know how hard it is to take 30 medications a day and go through the routine of dialysis three times a week. Despite that, we have never seen her give up. I must add that her husband has also never spoken negatively at any time, not even when she was critical in the ICU. He remained positive; he was travelling, doing his shows. And she had the inner strength to go through her medical problems and come out of it. It is an amazing story."

Right up to 2012, when something happened to change her mind, Medha was always scheduled to go back to New York for her kidney transplant. Couldn't doctors in Mumbai handle it?

Dr Kothari analysed her need to go abroad. "To be very frank, we don't have any experience in managing a cardiac transplant patient who is going in for a kidney transplant. She is the only multi-organ transplant patient I have dealt with in this country and probably not many doctors in the country have dealt with patients like her. Plus, the main reason is that her cardiac team is the main driving force for her treatment and she is comfortable with them. She spent almost a year at the hospital during the heart transplant and knows practically everyone there.

"A kidney transplant has become such a straightforward surgery that it is not very difficult for us to do it here. But obviously patient-comfort and patient-choice are big factors. If cost is not a concern then patients usually prefer to be treated by the care-givers who have looked after them for a long time. I have been totally supportive of her going to the US for her kidney transplant. It is a good decision because she is more comfortable there and she can always be in touch with me. Whenever she is in the US she sends me an SMS about every single medication that they may change. She keeps us in the loop and her doctors there are comfortable with that because after the kidney transplant, she will eventually return to India. So the long term follow-up is something that we will be doing. Therefore, it is a perfect decision to go back to where the heart transplant was done."

Although it sounded simple, the truth was that at any given time, Medha's condition could be listed as 'critical'. "She needs the kidney transplant because if she doesn't go for it, she will have to be on dialysis for the rest of her life and dialysis is not easy on a patient who has had a heart transplant, especially when there are blood pressure issues which are very difficult to manage," explained Dr Kothari.

"There are times when her BP is as low as 70/40, so it's not easy for the patient as well as the doctors treating her. She is just about managing to live; a transplant is the ideal treatment for kidney failure and we are hopeful that it will work out well for her."

He had reason to tread with caution as he explained, "On an average, we give a dialysis patient five to six years of survival, depending on the age and the medical problems they face. Someone who has had a cardiac transplant and is on dialysis would have a survival expectation which is less than that. Medha is pretty much aware of it but she has been willing to fight on. Because she wants to fight, we also look forward to her recovery and we want to try and give her the best possible treatment. Right now, a kidney transplant is the best option for her."

Dr Kothari may have been full of admiration. But when Medha was first put under his care, he had reason not to be too keen about his new patient. He agreed that he had his reservations because, "Celebrities are sometimes difficult to handle because most times they have expectations which far exceed our scientific knowledge and our capacity to handle them. But that has never been the case with Medha. Initially when Dr Kapadia handed me her case and said, 'You have to look after her now,' I was a little sceptical. A dialysis unit has so many patients and to differentiate between them or give special/separate care to one person is not possible in our day-to-day schedule. But surprisingly, Medha and Anup have never ever thrown their weight around. You will never hear that she has created a problem or made it difficult for my staff in the dialysis unit to manage. I have patients who belong to some corporate house or industrialists with influential connections, who keep calling me or have someone from the Hinduja family call me. But Medha has never used her celebrity status or her connections to jump the queue. It has never happened with her or with anybody from her family."

Courageous equanimity in desperate times makes Medha's story even more incredible. But among her colourful spectrum of well-wishers, all of whom at one time or the other feared that the end was near, there was one young woman who staunchly believed that Medha would sail home victorious because she had handed over her ailing friend to the care of "Matarani" (a goddess). Talking to Tripti Mukherjee was a further introduction to the fascinating variety of friends that Medha gathered at every stage of her life.

Tripti, the senior most disciple of Sangeet Martand Pandit Jasraj, is the director of Pandit Jasraj Institute in New York. Alternating between Mumbai and New York, this Indian classical vocalist and Medha were thrown together as disciples of Pandit Jasraj.

It was a familiar line you heard as Tripti also turned out to be one of Medha's "closest friends" whose first meeting with her left her, "Completely mesmerised by her beauty, her charming personality and her joyful nature."

But the *sur* (musical note) Tripti introduced to Medha's story was new as she had a distinctly new refrain in her narration, a totally different way of handling her friend's devastating disease. When Tripti first learnt of Medha's heart problem, she couldn't believe that she would have to go through such serious episodes. "But we took it as it came. You have no choice but to accept destiny. I am a complete devotee of Matarani and from the day I heard that Medha had this problem, I handed her over to my Matarani to take care of her. I had 100 per cent belief that Medha would come out of it and our belief got strengthened by looking at Medha's and Anupji's courage and faith in God."

When Medha got herself a new heart and was discharged from hospital, it was Radhika Tandon and Tripti Mukherjee who took her to her new home, her own apartment in New York. "It was really a very joyous day for all of us, for Medha's and Anupji's family, and all their friends. For the first few days, I was there alone with Medha and I took care of her every minute of the day. I tried to take care of her like my own child, like one takes care of a rose. I am really thankful to my Matarani for giving me an opportunity to do this seva for my dear friend."

Continuing with her own spiritual perspective, Tripti saw her friend take her medication with precision and witnessed her courageously face one medical upset after the other. But at no stage did she fear the worst. "Looking at Medha's and Anupji's positive attitude, I never feared for anything. We all know that problems will come, we have to overcome them and everything will be all right. Medha is an absolute fighter and a winner. I am sure if there had been any other person in Medha's place, she would have definitely lost this fight."

Characteristically, Tripti sourced Medha's success story to an inexplicable power. "One has to admit that it is only Anupji's trust, faith and belief in God, his support at every moment of Medha's life, his ultra-soft, caring nature and his ability to face life with a smiling face all the time, that has made all this possible. He is an amazing person and I feel God himself has come as Anupji to take care of her."

As Tripti evoked divinity to shower blessings on the twosome, she did come down to earth to state, "I want Medha to sing again."

It was the right juncture to introduce a completely new thought to Medha's treatment which came from renowned vocalist Pandit Jasraj. Medha not only looked up to him as her guruji but also learnt from him to respect all forms of music. Panditji, who begins every conversation with *Jai ho* (victory to thee), didn't quite remember when or where he first met Medha but what he was sure about was that she was always a very good student and "a beautiful listener".

Assessing Medha's abilities as a singer, Pandit Jasraj said, "When I said, she's a beautiful listener, it also means that she has deep knowledge of music. With Medha, I found that whatever she did was with great dedication. While she was learning music from me, I never felt that she was just passing time. She was a wonderful student."

Strangely, despite the high praise, Medha never did take to professional singing. Panditji had a simplistic explanation for that. "It all depends on God and destiny," said he.

Where Panditji's fresh thinking surfaced was when he explained his belief that her strength to rise to every difficult occasion came from, "Her music, her love of music and her love of life."

Her insatiable energy amused him because, "Medha used to come to the music class and after lunch, she used to teach yoga to all of us. That included me and all of us used to enjoy her yoga lessons."

His proximity to Medha made Pandit Jasraj accept Anup as, "My son-in-law. I love him immensely. And he loves Medha." He drew a parallel between Anup's devotion to Medha and the mythological Savitri who successfully pleaded with the gods for her husband's life. "Anup is the opposite (the male version) of Savitri. It is only Anupji's love which has brought Medha back to life. It is an unparalleled example of love."

"It is love, what else can it be?" echoed Talat Aziz. "It is not physical attraction, it is a very strong companionship. Otherwise, frankly speaking, there's no way they would be together like this. Any other person, perhaps, would have said, 'I have done enough,' and nobody would have held anything against him. But both of them are still going on. It is pure love, a very strong bond."

Is that what Medha's medical feat is ultimately? The triumph of true love over impossible, daunting odds?

14

Hope 2012

With three hernia operations, a bout of amnesia, dialysis up from three to four times a week and the much-awaited donor kidney still elusive, there was an incomprehensible cheer in the air.

"The year has begun well," said a contented Anup as he went up to receive a Padma Shri, the second in his family. His father had been similarly honoured by the President of India five years ago.

There was also sentimental satisfaction that close friend Jagjit Singh who had sung at Anup's birthday party in 2011, had spent his last two days with him in Dehradun. "He returned to Mumbai and went into hospital the next day. So Jagjit Singh's last concert was with me," disclosed Anup.

Professionally, Anup was chuffed over bagging the lead role in a film titled *Satya Sai Baba*. "I was only called to record a song for the film," Anup softly laughed. The filmmaker was toying with the idea of casting actor Makarand Deshpande as the saintly Sai Baba when Anup cajoled him to, "Take a close look at my face." The filmmaker looked, saw a glimpse of Sai Baba in Anup and, much to the singer's delight, cast him as his lead actor.

Medha had her own reasons to be happy. Mid-2012, she sent out a victory SMS to all her close friends that read: 'I want to share some wonderful news with you. Aryaman has scored 9 A Stars out of 9 subjects in his 10th Grade IGCSE Board exams. Valedictorian – first in school. Very satisfying feeling.'

Good things were happening to bring back the smiles and Medha was feeling better than she had for a long time. Despite no kidney transplant and the frequency of dialysis going up, the reasons for her spirits to soar and her body to respond with equal enthusiasm were quite a few:

The post-dialysis, low grade fever that had recurred and dragged her morale down all through 2011, had finally been ejected. It was done not by the usual pack of miracle workers in New York but in India's own Medanta in Gurgaon. "What took the doctors in New York two months to do in 2008, was achieved at Medanta in three weeks," Medha marvelled at the homegrown efficiency.

It led to a major change of heart. If and when the kidney transplant does happen, it won't be in New York anymore, Medha has put her faith in Dr Naresh Trehan's Medanta.

"I was at Medanta from December 2011 to Jan 2012," she methodically noted. "I went there for a kidney transplant evaluation but was feeling ill because of the fever. The doctors there said, 'Forget the transplant, we will first get rid of the infection.' The infection could have done me in, so they didn't let me get out till it went away. They did it with antibiotics after finding an infection in the abdominal cavity. Fluid collects in the cavity and the infection grows in that fluid. Tapping, which is invasive, could be causing the infection, so instead of tapping, I am now on dialysis four times a week."

It was unrelenting dialysis for the fourth year in a row and a spate of hernias, followed by haematoma (post-op clot) after every operation. Fortunately, Medha got rid of the haematoma in two months after the last hernia was surgically removed in mid-2012, instead of further medicating herself for it.

"So many other things happened. I also had an episode of amnesia in May 2012 which was absolutely disorienting.

"As long as it's just dialysis four times a week, I can deal with it," Medha accepted it as a part of routine life. "But beyond that, I don't want any more things to happen to me, like the fever. We know how to deal with it now, so I'm fine. But because my stomach lining is weak, I keep getting these hernias. I have had three hernia operations so far. One was caught in time, another one got strangulated and had to be done in an emergency last year in 2011 before Anupji's birthday. 2011 was low.

"In June-July 2012, I had gone to New York for my six-monthly clinic. It's a checkup that is not invasive, they just do an ECG etc. The heart came out fine but the hernia popped up and I was in a lot of pain. The surgeon said it was not strangulated but needed to be dealt with. I got the surgery done on June 28, just after my birthday. I had to stay in the US for a month. Now I have got my strength back, I am upbeat healthwise but nothing should happen to set me back. I have started going out again, we are socialising a lot. I even attended a Parent-Teacher meeting in Aryaman's school in a wheelchair. I get a little tired but I push myself to do it.

"I had gone to New York for a checkup but had the hernia surgery instead," she mused aloud. "Whenever I think of a kidney transplant, something else crops up. Somewhere I have begun to feel that these are omens telling me not to do a kidney transplant.

"But if I have to get it done, going to the US for a kidney transplant has been completely ruled out because they don't approve of our donors. Donors who were accepted here were rejected there. So if I have to do a kidney transplant I will go to Medanta in Gurgaon. I need a super-speciality hospital and

Medanta is really state-of-the-art. All this time I considered New York also because Dr Gass was very apprehensive of the anaesthesia. But something good came out of the hernia surgery that I underwent in 2012 because I went through the anaesthesia very well at Medanta. The anaesthetist has given me a whole two-page sheet of what he did, what medicines at what time, for how many minutes, etc."

With a hospital closer home and the bothersome anaesthesia sorted out, life was looking up indeed. But Medha continued to do a Hamlet, one day wanting to go in for a kidney transplant and the next day, preferring to make do with dialysis for as long as she could. "Half my mind is against the transplant, even the doctors are half-minded about it."

Meanwhile, Anup quietly continued his unusual love story by doing another role reversal – he observed Karva Chauth with the explanation, "Since Medha is ill and cannot keep the fast, I observe Karva Chauth for her long life and good health."

The couple crossed two more important landmarks in 2012. On August 5, 2012, Anup-Medha celebrated 18 years of marriage and the new heart ticking inside Medha turned 11 in December.

There was more cheer in store on January 17, 2013. With Medha firmly by his side, Anup took on the eminently well-suited role of Editor of the Indian edition of *Tathaastu* ('so be it', in Sanskrit), an internationally published wellness magazine. And mom organised a big party for Aryaman's 17th birthday as he inched towards adulthood on Jan 26.

Health, wealth and wellness? So be it.